Praise for *Boredom Busters*

"Love, love, love this book by Katie Powell! As someone who uses brain research as the foundation of all I do, Katie hits the nail on the head with this one. New and novel ideas turn that worksheet into an engaging power tool, along with variations! Her book made me think about wanting to be back in the classroom again, so imagine how students (and you) will feel!"

—**LaVonna Roth**, creator and founder of Ignite Your S.H.I.N.E.®, @LaVonnaRoth

"*Boredom Busters* is literally a treasure trove of ideas and activities to help any teacher stay engaged with students, even when the coffee maker is on the fritz! Katie captures the reality of not only being a teacher but a real person who has an entire life outside of the school day that totally impacts our teaching flow. Life happens, and when it does, you definitely need *Boredom Busters* at your fingertips to keep the magic going in your classroom!"

—**Marlena Gross-Taylor**, social commerce entrepreneur, founder @EduGladiators, author, speaker, edleader

"*Boredom Busters* is a creative masterpiece! Katie Powell views fun as the baking soda—the active ingredient in learning. Any teacher who wants to create a joyful, collaborative learning space should read this book immediately and implement her ideas. She's an experienced teacher who understands the 'real' versus the 'ideal' and knows teachers have logistical, financial, and time constraints. She also understands kids' varying needs and attention spans, and she gets their sense of humor. For instance, she knows exactly how a sixth grader will react to the word *balls*, and suggests using the phrase *learning spheres* instead. I've seen Powell present at conferences, and she's the real deal—a gifted, energetic, innovative teacher who recognizes that everyone brings their own unique strengths to the table. Whether she's teaching or writing, Powell leads with humility, wit, wisdom, and empathy. There's no judgment here—only solid, practical, road-tested tips that will revolutionize your classroom."

—**Phyllis Fagell**, author of *Middle School Matters*, *Washington Post* contributor, and school counselor

"From the first page, *Boredom Busters* comes out swinging like a wrecking ball, offering practical, action-oriented upgrades to help shatter any typical worksheet, lecture, or homework assignment you can possibly imagine. *Boredom Busters* is a dynamic playbook of teaching strategies that can add life, rigor, and relevance to any lesson plan with minimal prep and zero added cost. Like the Kool-Aid man exploding through the wall of your kitchen, Katie Powell's high-energy approach to education is packed with all sorts of instant excitement—making it an outstanding resource for teachers of any grade level."

—**John Meehan**, author of *EDrenaline Rush*

"Katie blends a desire to allow engagement to flourish with realistic expectations to create actual solutions and encourage outside-the-box thinking. Whether you are a new teacher looking for activities to add to your instructional tool chest or a veteran teacher looking to spice up your classroom, *Boredom Busters* offers you support in your craft."

—**Phil Strunk**, founder of #WALEDchat and host of *Edusations*

"Get ready to fly through this book and land right into a more engaged class! Katie Powell's *Boredom Busters* leap right out of the book and into action in your classroom. The only thing that got me to put the book down was to get ready for the next class. There is such comfort for a teacher knowing kids are going to leave with a happy heart and a full head. With such practical ideas, this is a must buy for anyone!"

—**Michael Matera**, speaker, author, teacher

TRANSFORM WORKSHEETS, LECTURES, AND GRADING INTO ENGAGING, MEANINGFUL, LEARNING EXPERIENCES

Katie Powell

Boredom Busters

Published by Dave Burgess Consulting, Inc.
San Diego, CA
DaveBurgessConsulting.com

Editing, cover design, and interior design by My Writers' Connection
Author photo by Linsey Hannum Photography

Library of Congress Control Number: 2019945827
Paperback ISBN: 978-1-949595-68-0
Ebook ISBN: 978-1-949595-69-7

First Printing: August 2019

Contents

Part 1

WHERE WE BEGIN

Chapter 1

That Time I Learned I Actually Don't Know Everything

I was so arrogant. Of course, I didn't think so at the time. At the time, it was just the unbridled exuberance and passion of a new teacher. But looking back, yeah, it was arrogance. I started my teaching career as a middle grades special education teacher. I quickly discovered that a middle grades special education student is one of the saddest creatures on the face of this planet.

Okay, before you start writing me impassioned letters, let me explain. The act of struggling hurts. It leaves the struggler uncertain. Feeling like one doesn't quite measure up, over and over again, day after day, wears the struggler down like a steady stream of water against a stone. The impact is powerful. And lasting. Some of my students in those early years had been struggling for a long time. Kids like that decide school, learning, and intelligence just aren't for them, and they check out. They see school as something they just have to get through until they're released to pursue whatever kind of life they want for themselves. It broke my heart to see this, and it burned me up.

I learned that to reach these students, I had to essentially hide the learning so it didn't feel like school. Yes, I know we're supposed to make our learning targets explicit, let them clearly see the goal for which they're aiming, but that's not what I mean. I mean the lessons I planned couldn't feel exactly like the school experiences they'd failed at so far.

I'm naturally creative and don't mind taking risks (if for a good cause), so trying to create something different—something better—actually seemed like an exciting challenge. I planned lessons that felt like competitions, games, projects, or passionate debates. I utilized technology at a time where classroom technology was still very much a sparkly new toy. I made everything as hands-on and explorative as I possibly could. We learned in groups, on the floor, under tables, and beyond our classroom. We made videos and websites. We were loud.

And it worked.

Those students who had defined themselves by their failures—who assumed they *were* failures and somehow defective or broken—started to have fun. They started to enjoy class. Most importantly, they started to learn.

A lot.

We developed a classroom culture that was safe, where they felt they belonged. And even though many of the things I tried in those first years failed, I am confident those students saw that I was trying, and they responded to that.

In addition to teaching my own classes, I spent the remainder of my day providing inclusion support in other teachers' classrooms. That is where the arrogance came in.

I would see those students I had worked *so hard* to reach revert to disconnected states or even insolence in other classrooms, little more than furniture at best and significant discipline issues at worst. I'd watch teachers teach, period after period, hour after hour, day after day, as "sage on the stage," talking *at* students and then assigning work for which they required the students to remain silent. I sat those hours with the students, my own butt getting numb, my own concentration struggling. Frustrated and filled with new-teacher self-importance, I was furious.

Why weren't these teachers doing more to reach the students? Why were they ignoring such clear needs? Why didn't they know better? I declared them "bad" teachers in my own heart and mind and looked down my slightly upturned and very freckled nose at them.

Y'all, I'm so glad that's not the end of my story.

With experience, and perhaps age, comes a measure of wisdom. As I continued serving in other teachers' classrooms, I eventually learned that all of them loved their content. Passionately. At times, it was the deep love of their content that created the disconnect I saw between the way they taught and the way "my" students needed to learn. These passionate teachers expected the wonder and glory they felt about their content to be enough to engage students.

But let's face it: Often, it's not.

Witnessing these teachers, period after period, day after day, I started to see how they loved their craft. They loved students! They were expert teachers giving their best every day.

This went from a flickering realization to a full-blown-cartoon-anvil-dropped-on-my-head *aha*-moment when I started to plan "co-taught" lessons with another teacher on my team. Cammie taught writing and passionately loved her content. She admired her students, especially the naturally academically adept ones. She attended conferences, read books, and fretted over her lessons. I didn't know any of that until I started planning lessons with her.

We had worked together for years, but we had never just talked frankly about our craft of teaching. Sure, she'd vent about students, or we'd talk through how we were going to comply with the latest administrative directive, but our working relationship hadn't gone any deeper than that. I had assumed that because her lessons didn't strike me as particularly engaging, she didn't care about reaching *all* students. It was clear she liked some—the easy kids, those who sat up straight, raised their hands, turned their essays in on time—but what about "my" kids? The sullen ones? The ones with their heads down? The ones more likely to crack a joke than risk making a mistake in front of their peers? I assumed she didn't like them—or worse, didn't care about them.

What an assumption to make.

As our working relationship grew, as we planned lessons side-by-side, I started to understand that the reality for her—and for most of us, really—is that it's far more complicated than just liking some kids and not others. She framed it this way: "Katie, I know I have to teach *all* students. I just don't know *how*. I don't know how to reach the kids that don't even want to be here!"

What's behind liking some kids and not liking others is really the sense of powerlessness many teachers feel. Those kids who don't even want to be at school challenge us. We're not sure how to reach them, let alone how to teach them to diagram sentences or simplify expressions. I learned through those lesson planning sessions that this teacher was reading article after article and losing sleep over how to reach these kids. And she kept coming up empty.

Insert metaphorical foot into metaphorical mouth here.

All that time, I'd been looking down that nose I described earlier when I could have been using my new-teacher passion and enthusiasm to help my fellow teachers with their needs and support them.

Respect them.

Empower them with ideas.

Partner with them to reach *our* students.

And I'd blown it.

That teacher and I wound up working together really well. We learned to play to each other's strengths and planned lessons where she would take part of the class for expert instruction while I took others for hands-on activities to support the learning goals, and then the kids would switch, allowing them to benefit from what we did best.

And it worked.

We both were so encouraged and excited.

Working with this teacher was a turning point experience for me. It wasn't quite the birth of *Worksheet Busters*, but it was the genesis of my understanding of the need for them. I understood, albeit embarrassingly late, that teachers *want* to be good teachers. Sometimes we just don't know how. Maybe we're afraid. Maybe we were taught to teach one way, and now all the educational experts are saying that's not enough. Maybe we love our content so dog-gone much that we just can't fathom a student not being enthralled by it. Maybe we feel hemmed in by a lack of time or resources.

But all of us—*all of us*—want to be good teachers.

I have spent more than a dozen years of my teaching career supporting other teachers' instruction as a special education teacher, a Title 1 teacher, an instructional coach, and even a couple short stints as an instructional assistant. With that background, I wound up with plenty of time to exercise my newfound respect for my fellow teachers. I started to break apart and analyze what I did in my own classroom, to distill it into a replicable formula, and see if I could teach other teachers to do it.

I bet you can predict how that worked.

It didn't. And you know why.

Other teachers don't need to teach the way *I* teach. They need to teach the way *they* teach.

Again, cartoon anvil. It's much more emphatic than a light bulb, that's for sure.

So I went back to the drawing board. I went back to my formula. I studied teachers, and I discovered a few things. Building on the foundation that all teachers want to be good teachers, I found . . .

- Teachers are already accomplished experts.
- Some teachers are afraid of active learning.
- But all teachers trust worksheets.

Now, stick with me on that last point. I know some of you have eagerly and excitedly left your textbooks behind, stopped assigning homework, or made other revolutionary changes. There are many exciting, challenging movements in education these days, but even anti-worksheet teachers at some point give students problems to practice. At some point, we present questions for students to answer. We all do! And when you glance up from your own nose, freckled or otherwise, consider those teachers who are afraid of active learning. Those teachers who have taught the same way their whole careers. Those teachers who suddenly feel affronted, disrespected, or discouraged by the insistence that their expert teaching is somehow now not enough. Do those teachers trust worksheets? You bet they do.

Worksheets are readily available. They come with our textbook adoptions as paperbacks of blackline masters or in binders with shiny covers. Because they came with the textbook, we trust their quality and depth. We trust that they'll adequately mirror the test questions and help our students prepare for success. We can print them off the internet with a swipe of our copy machine card. Our file cabinets are full of them. We don't have to scrounge to find them or spend our time creating them. Worksheets give our students plenty of problems to practice. Worksheets are safe. As a profession, we continue to use worksheets because they provide a pre-packaged and reasonably reliable way for our students to practice concepts and skills.

Those teachers I worked with early in my career used worksheets often. But those worksheets weren't working for all of our students. That sheet of paper may have provided a bank of problems appropriate in content and difficulty, aligned to the district curriculum. It may have felt safe to that teacher and have been readily available and easy to assign and grade. But that flat page likely did little to engage struggling students. Recently I participated in the Remaking Middle School Summit in Washington, DC. A panel of students shared their experiences to open the event. One sixth-grade student said, "I hate school. All we ever do are handouts. Handouts, handouts, handouts. I only go to school so I can go to my after-school program." That's a narrative we have to change. We needed something more. But more is scary. Worksheets are safe. Something different is uncertain. Unpredictable. Risky.

If my students were struggling to accept a new concept, were afraid to step out and risk failure, to take something to the next step, I wouldn't look down on them. I'd meet them at their present level and stand alongside them to help them get where they needed to go. I'd do so with grace, patience, compassion, and respect. Why had I been doing anything less with my fellow teachers all those years?

So, seeking to meet teachers where they were, I decided worksheets were the ubiquitous place to start. Trusted. Universal. Available.

But just the place to start, not the end of the story.

Utilizing the formula I'd broken down from my own teaching style and my research into engagement and diverse learning needs, I started to build some strategies, all starting with worksheets, that could engage even our most stoic of students. I carefully crafted and fine-tuned these activities to be adaptable, so any teacher could apply them to his or her own content and within his or her own teaching style, so it wasn't about trying to teach like me (or anyone else for that matter). Instead, it was about empowering teachers to educate effectively within their own expert approaches. I made them scalable—teachers who remained uncomfortable with lots of movement, materials, or steps could use them one way (and still be very successful) while teachers who were more comfortable with movement and activity could expand the framework in other ways. And because I'm a teacher on a teacher's salary married to a minister on a minister's salary, I made them all free or very, very cheap to make.

I also happen to have some unique health challenges. (Go ahead and Google "Ehlers-Danlos syndrome" and "gastroparesis" sometime. Yeah, it's fun.) I'm fortunate to be healthy enough to work full-time and do so well, but my energy and wellness are limited. And my family deserves some of me too. So I *have* to preserve myself to still be some kind of good for them. I can't give it *all* to school, but I still want to be a good teacher—no, I want to be *great*—so my ideas have to maximize resources I already have or can easily get. They have to be simple to make, set up, and implement.

Imagine this scenario: It's Monday morning. Fresh off a weekend spent with family, fuzzy socks, a healthy dose of sunshine, and an unapologetically unhealthy amount of screen time, you're excited about the lesson you've planned. You printed, laminated, and cut your materials ahead of time, and they're all laid out just so. You even took the time to decorate the room in support of the lesson's theme. You've planned interaction, tech integration, and a check for understanding, so you know who you need to meet with tomorrow. You've got bell-work posted, music playing, and are stationed at the door, ready to greet your students with a smile or a trendy, personalized, handshake routine. Your clothes are pressed, and your shoes fashionable. Today, you rock.

And then you've got to do it again tomorrow.

And Wednesday.

And Thursday.

And by then, you're tapped out. Your coffeemaker is on the fritz, brewing rust-colored water instead of coffee, spurting it across your counter—and your slightly rumpled shirt—as you rush out the door, praying you beat that red Ford Focus that happens to drive the same morning route you do, just at about twelve miles per hour slower than you'd like to go. Family time has amounted to chauffeuring one kid to soccer, another to theater, and entertaining the other while getting the hole in your tire patched since your car knows exactly when you don't have time for these kinds of shenanigans and has conspired with the coffeemaker to teach you some kind of lesson about patience. You gave up on the fashionable shoes and switched to tennis shoes by Tuesday afternoon. The morning staff meeting ran over, so now you can either post your bell-work or take a bathroom break, so you sacrifice the bell ringer in the name of relieving your bladder since you know it will be exactly four hours and twenty-three minutes until you get another chance. After the tech department emailed yesterday, letting you know exactly which sites a cluster of students managed to visit during class, you've vowed to pretend it's 1983 and go fully analog. Tuesday's small groups turned into a contest in which the students you needed to work with (and the rest of the class) competed to see who could be off-task in the most creative ways possible, so now you've given up on small groups in favor of crowd control. Today . . . today you are knee-deep in The Thursday Problem.

We've all been there. Sometimes we have precisely the right activity for the objective, and we can craft a truly memorable and valuable learning experience. But other times, for a variety of reasons, we find that our lesson plan amounts to "page 117."

Yeah.

The Thursday Problem.

That's where Worksheet Busters belong. When you can craft a learning experience perfectly suited to your objective, you should. But when you find yourself facing The Thursday Problem (even if it's Monday), Worksheet Busters are a sanity-saving way to engage your students in deep, meaningful learning. They are activity frameworks that can be adapted for any content at any time. They can become classroom routines as much as passing out papers or lining up for dismissal. In fact, teachers from primary grades to college campuses are using Worksheet Busters. Many Worksheet Busters require no special materials. All are easy to make or set up. And all bring added depth and value to traditional worksheets.

Can worksheets be fun? You bet they can. What about homework? Or lectures? If you keep reading, you'll find out lots of ways they can. But fun for fun's sake is never enough. We aren't hired to be fun. This isn't a circus, birthday party, or stage production. This is school. We are hired to be teachers with expert understanding of the standards and a masterful ability to impart that understanding to our students (and everything you know that involves).

Fun is a very effective tool to leverage. If students are having fun, they are interested, connected, and engaged. The walls they've built against school and learning come down. They may even start to *like* school. Great things will follow, which create the ideal conditions for meaningful engagement.

Fun is a tool we leverage. It's effective. But it's not the end goal.

In addition to being fun (or novel or weird or unexpected), Worksheet Busters are deep. They take the original experience of whatever worksheet you start with and drive the learning deeper, requiring higher-order thinking skills or a whole different depth of knowledge (DOK). In other words, massive learning bang for your very little (or non-existent) buck.

Imagine your students' reactions when you unfurl a giant game board across the floor or dump out a bag of ball-pit balls, tell them to fold their worksheet into a paper airplane, or give them permission to dance across the classroom. Curious? They will be too. And they'll want to come back for more tomorrow.

Chapter 2

Where Do You Fall Between Vomit and Tomorrow?

When I present Worksheet Busters, I close with an exit ticket that asks participants to evaluate where they fall on a continuum between *vomit* and *tomorrow*.

Rate yourself on a scale of one to ten, ten meaning, "Gosh, Katie, I'm going to use some of these activities tomorrow!" and one meaning, "Thinking about getting kids moving around the room like this makes me break out in a cold sweat and feel like I'm going to vomit."

(Vomit) 1—2—3—4—5—6—7—8—9—10 (Tomorrow!)

This scale provides feedback for me as to how empowered and equipped participants feel to implement Worksheet Busters in their own classrooms after our hour or so together. Now, before we move forward with this book, I think it's equally valuable to take a moment to evaluate your own comfort level with active learning. Every idea you'll encounter in this book is scalable, so you'll find a place to start, even if you fall closer to the *vomit* end of the continuum. If you're already an out-of-the-box teacher, you'll find plenty of options to take each idea anywhere you want to go (and then spark your own creativity to take it even further).

Let me reiterate—you are an expert teacher. There is not one "best practice" or one best way to teach. One of my favorite things about our profession is that there are a variety of ways to do it well. What a wonderful thing! Many expert teachers are doing amazing things in their classrooms, no two teachers doing it exactly alike, yet they are still doing it equally well. Maybe you rely on your textbook. Maybe you haven't touched a textbook in years. Maybe you have file cabinets full of blackline masters. Maybe you are totally paperless. Maybe you lecture. Maybe you personalize learning.

But all of us have to engage our students.

Several years ago, Indiana was one of many states to move away from the idea of tenure. For a long time, a teacher's job security and pay were essentially based on how long they'd taught at that school. With the advent of teacher evaluation systems, though, teachers found that their salaries and job security were tied to their performance. Although the evaluative process differs from state to state or from district to district, student engagement is found in all of them.

Okay, so let's be honest—I haven't checked them *all*. I'm operating on a reasonable assumption here. Go ahead and look at yours. Indiana uses the RISE 2.0 rubric. Competency 2.3 reads, "Engage students in academic content." The descriptors for effective and highly effective ratings include statements like, "teacher provides ways to engage with content that significantly promote student mastery of the objective," "three-quarters or more of students are actively engaged in content at all times and not off-task," "teacher provides multiple ways, as appropriate, of engaging with content," and "students work hard and are deeply active rather than passive or receptive."

In short, we have to engage students.

Philip Schlecty's

Levels of Engagement

Drawn by @sylviaduckworth

ATTENTION + COMMITMENT = LEVEL OF ENGAGEMENT

Attention	Commitment	Level of Engagement
HIGH ATTENTION	HIGH COMMITMENT	ENGAGEMENT · The student associates the task with a result or product that has meaning and value for the student. The student will persist in the face of difficulty and will learn at high and profound levels.
HIGH ATTENTION	LOW COMMITMENT	STRATEGIC COMPLIANCE · The task has little inherent or direct value to the student, but the student associates it with outcomes or results that do have value to the student (such as grades). Student will abandon work if extrinsic goals are not realized and will not retained what is learned.
LOW ATTENTION	LOW COMMITMENT	RITUAL COMPLIANCE · The student is willing to expend whatever effort is needed to avoid negative consequences. The emphasis is on meeting the minimum requirements. The student will learn at low and superficial levels.
NO ATTENTION	LOW COMMITMENT	RETREATISM · The student is disengaged from the task and does not attempt to comply with its demands, but does not try to disrupt the work or substitute other activities for it. The student does not participate and learns little or nothing from the task.
DIVERTED ATTENTION	NO COMMITMENT	REBELLION · The student refuses to do the work, acts in ways to disrupt others, or substitutes tasks / activities to which he or she is committed. Student develops poor work and sometimes negative attitudes towards formal education and intellectual tasks.

And compliance is not engagement.

Just because a kid is quietly occupying his seat, pencil in hand, worksheet in front of him, does not mean he's engaged.

But let's assume for a moment that she *is* engaged in the worksheet. Let's imagine she is fully engrossed in answering those questions. That would be enough, right?

Nope.

Now we have to consider depth of knowledge. Not only must students be engaged, but they must engage in work that is rigorous and challenging. The Indiana RISE 2.0 rubric Competency 2.6 reads, "Develop Higher Level of Understanding through Rigorous Instruction and Work." Descriptions of what that looks like include: "teacher is highly effective at developing a higher level of understanding through rigorous instruction and work," "lesson is accessible and challenging to all students," and "students are able to answer higher-level questions with meaningful responses." What does "rigorous work" look like?

One common descriptor of rigor is depth of knowledge (DOK). There are four levels of DOK. Though rigor and DOK are not precisely synonymous, an oversimplified explanation is that work with a higher DOK tends to be more rigorous. DOK 1 includes verbs such as *calculate*, *define*, *describe*, *explain*, *identify*, *label*, *list*, and *match*.

Take a moment and pull out a worksheet. Or Google one. Take a look at the directions. Find the verb. Notice anything?

Although I hesitate to paint all worksheets with such a broad brush, the vast majority of worksheets fall squarely in DOK 1. It is not bad to spend time in DOK 1. But we can't camp out there. We must take students further. Deeper. Consider the verbs of DOK level three: critique, defend, interpret, justify.

Worksheets rarely require that, but Worksheet Busters do.

I hope you will find inspiration within an idea in this book, or maybe several, that will spark your own curiosity and excitement as a teacher. I hope reading this book leaves you empowered and equipped to authentically engage your students. But whether you try Worksheet Busters or not, the reality is that we are all still held to the expectation that we engage our students in meaningful, challenging learning. For some of us, that's scary. It means doing things differently than we've done them before. It may mean trying new things. But what if you try a new idea and it fails?

What would we tell a student who has failed? We are so madly in love with the ideas of grit and a growth mindset for our students, but why do we assume that doesn't apply to us? We tell our students that failure is all part of learning, the power of "yet," but we expect perfection out of ourselves.

I get it. Failure isn't comfortable. Educators tend to be a bit control-oriented and perfectionistic, but I have some thoughts about that.

Perhaps experiencing failure from time to time will help us remain sensitive to how our students feel, and we will be better teachers for it.

Truly great things can happen from failure.

If you try an idea and it fails, you can better plan for next time. It could mean it wasn't the best fit for that content or your class. It could be that it was new and unfamiliar, leaving you uncomfortable. Maybe your students picked up on that. All of that's feedback. Take it. Use it. Keep going. Keep trying. Not every idea that fails should be rejected outright. But even if an idea does deserve to be rejected, there are too many powerful ideas out there to let that stop you. Let's not accept that the way we've always done it is good enough just because it's safe. In the words of Shuri, the sister of Marvel's Black Panther, "Just because something works doesn't mean it can't be improved."

If you're worried what your principal will think if she walks in to see a less-than-perfect lesson, have a conversation. Reference the professional rubric and your own desire to grow as an educator, to be the best possible teacher for your students and school. Share your vision, but also share your fears. Allow your principal the opportunity to come alongside you and support you. I doubt there are many principals out there who would say, "You know, I really don't want you to be better. I think mediocre teaching is good enough."

And if your principal *does* say that, it may be time to spruce up that resume. My friend, there are greener pastures.

Let's address some specific concerns together.

Chapter 3

I See You Crossing Your Arms

When I present Worksheet Busters, the most common question I'm asked is how to handle *that* student or *that* class. You know the one. The one that requires special sub plans. The one you pop a couple ibuprofen before. The one that leaves you raiding your desk-drawer stash of chocolate. Here's what happens: I introduce Worksheet Busters with Paper Airplanes, Musical Desks, and Hungry Hippos. Participants are smiling, energetic, and excited. They take eager notes and talk animatedly with their colleagues.

And then there's this moment: The smile droops. The eyebrows lower. The pen stills. And the participant will lean back and cross her arms.

And I know she's just thought of *that* student or *that* class. She's thinking these ideas won't work for *that* student or *that* class. So she's cautious. Even skeptical. That spark of empowerment and inspiration is quickly snuffed out.

So let's not wait until after Paper Airplanes, Musical Desks, or Hungry Hippos to address this. I'll cut you off at the pass. Before you can lean back and cross your arms, bear with me. Keep that pen in hand. Let's figure this out together.

We all have some students who exhibit hard-to-manage behaviors. Or even whole classes with a challenging dynamic. Some kids come to us with so much baggage that reaching them even with safe work is challenging. When we think of these students as we consider new ideas, what we're really feeling is fear. Our fear. Fear of what will happen if we try something new, something risky, with those students. We're afraid that if we struggle to manage them even under the safest of circumstances, how will we ever manage them if we get them up and moving? We fear loss of control.

One of the entrance tickets I use in my sessions asks participants to draw pictures or symbols to represent what holds us back from including more active learning in our lessons. My favorite response was a stick figure on fire.

We're not sure how it will happen.

But we're sure it will.

So let's take a moment to address that fear. Let's name it. What we're afraid of is a loss of control, that not all students will behave, remain quiet, and stay seated and compliant.

Now let's challenge it. Are those students already behaving, remaining quiet, staying seated, and being compliant?

No, I didn't think so.

So why *not* try something new? I'm not naive—I know there are a number of reasons those students are hard to manage. I know there's no one-size-fits-all cause. There's definitely no one-size-fits-all solution. Anyone who claims to have one is selling snake oil. But I'd like to challenge you to consider what would happen if you surprised those very students with novelty.

Go ahead; picture one of those students. A specific one. Pull his name and face to the forefront of your mind. Feel all the emotions you feel regarding her. Hold it there. Now picture how this student would look if he walked into your room and saw the desks pushed aside and a giant board game spread out across the floor. What would her face look like? What would he say? For a moment, you'd have him. He'd be surprised and curious because it's *different*. Chances are high that this student has decided school—even your class—isn't for her. She's biding her time until she can get out. But today he walked in and it was . . . different. For a moment, whatever emotions she arrived with are paused, put aside, and she feels curiosity instead. That, my friends, is powerful. Use it.

Remember, surprising my students with learning that didn't feel like "school" to them was where these ideas started. Y'all, I didn't have to figure out how to make these ideas work for kids like that. I crafted these ideas *for* kids like that.

So let's try it. Let's bank on the idea that his moment of curiosity is a powerful place to start. For a moment, her guard will be down. It might be a great chance to engage that one student.

But then we live in the real world. That moment of curiosity isn't going to guarantee perfect behavior. In fact, you might now be picturing him picking up the giant board game and crawling beneath it. Maybe you're imagining her taking advantage of the pushed-back desks to push a classmate into the pile. The reality is, we have to plan for what comes after the curiosity.

And we can do that.

The Physical Space

Most Worksheet Busters are designed to work with literally any room layout. Others require some clear floor space. Before introducing a new idea, think about the layout of your room. What are the traffic patterns? Where are the hot spots? Does the physical space of your room provide for clear space? Are you bound by constraints that leave you without an open area? Pick ideas that work with the physical layout of your room and the needs of your students within it. And don't forget that there may be learning spaces in your building that *aren't* your classroom. If you really want to try an idea and don't have the space, take the learning beyond the walls of your room.

Time Management

We constantly feel short on time as teachers. We are pressed upon by the weight of all the standards we need to teach in a year. And, inevitably, the bell will ring before we're ready. But these ideas are designed to be scalable to fit any length of time you have available. From three-minute Lecture Busters to full-class-session versions of various Worksheet Busters, you decide what time you have available. Active learning does not have to be time consuming. But we also worry about the amount of time it takes to *plan* active learning. Take heart. Many Worksheet Busters can be deployed with no special preparation and no materials beyond a question or worksheet you would be using already.

Behavior

I recommend you lay out your expectations clearly before an activity even starts. Display them. Talk about them. Whether it's the rule that they hold their paper airplane till you explicitly tell them to launch it or that they hold their learning sphere quietly in their hands until you collect it, be clear and direct about what you want.

And then be ready for when they don't comply.

My standard is to have a paper copy of the worksheet or question set ready, and if a student violates a clearly defined and clearly understood expectation, I have him or her complete the worksheet alone without participating in the activity with the rest of the class. They're still getting the same opportunity to learn. (Okay, so it's a bit shallower without the added depth of the Worksheet Buster activity, but we've given that same worksheet in the past with full peace of mind, right?) While the rest of us laugh and learn through play, that student sits, a bit apart from us, completing the questions all alone.

Maybe that feels cruel. I assure you, it's not. Watch them. They'll gaze over at the rest of the group with a look of longing. Sure, they may be mad. They may pout or spout off a bit. That's human. But then they'll witness the value of the activity you intended them to participate in. They'll see why it matters firsthand.

And next time, they'll probably follow the rules.

Now, again, you know your kids. You know if that approach is appropriate for them or not. There may be times it's more appropriate to pull that student aside for a redirect. Or maybe she legitimately didn't understand the rules. Or his impulse control is just so poor that he literally can't resist. You are the expert. The process I described is my typical go-to, and I can tell you I've rarely had to remove a student more than once. Heck, I rarely have to remove a student even once.

The honest reality is that most students *want* to learn like this. Most students want the fun, the novelty, the movement, the socialization. So when we offer it, they eagerly gobble it up.

I will readily admit I'm not an expert on classroom management. I establish routines and expectations, and we practice them often. I have a gamified system of rewards and consequences, and I try to stick to it. But this isn't my strength.

And yet, I use Worksheet Busters, and they work. Let me say that again: I am not an expert classroom manager. You're probably better than I am! And I can do this. So you can too.

What if We're Afraid?

If you're still afraid of what will happen when you try a new idea, still afraid that stick figure will burst into flames, you should talk to your students. Tell them you want to be a better teacher for them, that it's what they deserve. Tell them you're afraid of what will happen if you get them up to move more, play more learning games, leave the safety of structured seatwork behind for a bit. Ask them if they want to try new things with you. Will they partner with you? Can you work together to try out some new things? They love opportunities like this. It makes them feel important.

And if an idea *does* fail, you will have a class full of students ready to perform the post-mortem with you, helping you diagnose and solve the problem.

Honor your students by giving them this opportunity. Tag them in. Give them the chance to step up.

Don't Forget Your Colleagues

If someone on your team is more comfortable or adept at a teaching skill you're uncertain about, ask to observe them in action. Talk to them about how they learned to do what they do well. You get to benefit from their experience. They've fallen into all the pits before you. They've found every weakness. They've bruised their shins so you can walk through more safely and successfully.

Ask them to observe you or maybe even co-teach a lesson with you. Pick one idea and try it with one class, this colleague by your side. Talk to them after. Reflect. And learn together.

Start Small

If you're still nervous or unsure, the safest place to start is small. One idea, one class. Set aside just ten minutes. Try one round of one idea.

See how it goes.

Then go from there.

Now that we've addressed your fears and your arms are uncrossed, pen still in hand, lean in.

Get ready.

Here we go.

Part 2

WORKSHEET BUSTERS

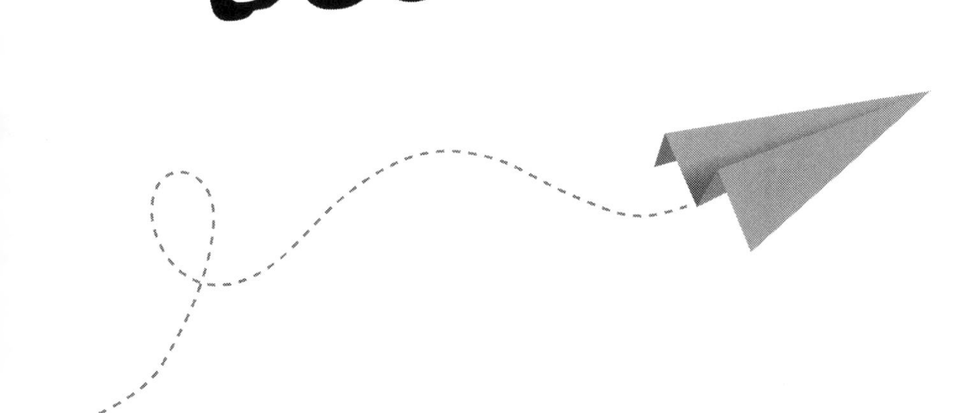

Chapter 4

No Prep, No Materials

Paper Airplanes

The Gist: Students fold their worksheets into paper airplanes and fly them around the room, then take the nearest one and work on that worksheet, continuing where the last student left off.

Why Do It: Students rarely care much about the work they do on a traditional worksheet. Playing Paper Airplanes gets them up and moving, increases engagement and motivation, and generally breaks up the monotony of a regular school day. This activity also gives students an equal opportunity to solve problems and evaluate answers, increasing the rigor of a typical worksheet. Students have the opportunity to engage in social learning, sharing their thoughts with and learning from one another throughout the activity. Paper Airplanes requires no special materials or preparation. Besides, most kids *love* making paper airplanes but rarely have their teachers' approval to do so. Making a worksheet into a paper airplane feels just a bit taboo or rebellious, and it's downright fun.

Materials

- Worksheet

Set Up

- Make one copy of the worksheet for each student.

To Play

1. Have each student put their name on their worksheet and do the first problem.
2. When they finish that problem, have them fold their worksheet into an airplane.

NOTE: Paper balls fly just fine. Rockstar teacher Erin Scholes's class deemed these "UFOs." Some also call this a "snowball fight."

3. Students stand and hold their paper airplanes. (Make it clear their airplanes do not leave their fingers until you tell them to do so.) At your signal, they throw their airplane toward the other side or the middle of the room.

4. Students grab the nearest worksheet and do one more problem. They should initial every problem they do throughout the rest of the game.

NOTE: Students who find extra airplanes should hold them high in the air, so others who are still looking can easily find them. Although teachers fear the loss of time, I've used Paper Airplanes in rooms of hundreds of educators, and we've found all the airplanes and returned to our seats in minutes. Kids are excellent at looking under desks and tracking down renegade projectiles.

5. Repeat steps two through four until the end of playing time or until the worksheet is finished.
6. Students get their original worksheet back and evaluate all the answers contributed on it. Have them leave the original answer but mark any corrections below or beside the original answer. This allows you to track students' understanding across the worksheets. Make it clear that students will be graded on what they submit on their worksheet, so it is up to them to catch and correct mistakes.

Caution and Tips

- Make it clear that these airplanes are not weapons.
- Make your expectations very clear as to *when*, *how*, and *where* the airplanes can be thrown.
- You'll find some of your students are paper aeronautical engineers. This is their chance to shine. Acknowledge their expertise. Allow them to help others. Watch as students ooh and ah as these kids' constructions fly in crisp, straight lines or loop animatedly through the air.
- Paper airplane tutorials are available online. You can post directions in the room and link to sites and videos for your students, etc.

- Spot check that students are initialing every problem they do. You'll want to hold students accountable if they don't give real effort and track how they're doing. This also allows you to follow up with students who may need additional academic support.
- If students cannot behave according to your expectations during the activity, they can be sent back to their desk to complete the entire worksheet on their own.

Variations

- Instruct students to do the next problem in sequential order (making sure that every student gets practice with every problem) or allow free choice of which problem to do (This allows uncertain students to do a problem they might be more comfortable with.).
- To save time, students can complete multiple problems each turn, or you can stop the game early and have students finish the worksheet on their own after they evaluate the answers on their page.
- Paper Airplanes can be used with essay questions or multistep problems too. Students do one step or work for a limited amount of time, pass, and then continue the problem or essay topic they receive.
- Students can all be working on the same question set or passing different questions.
- This activity can be used for trade-to-grade or to evaluate student work. Students grade the airplane they receive or pass their work and contribute one response of constructive feedback each round.
- Not using a worksheet? Display or share a question each round and have students answer on notebook paper.

- Have great rapport with your class? Let yourself be a target. A circular trash can lid makes a great Captain America-style shield.

Differentiation Ideas

- Need varied, leveled, scaffolded, adapted, or accommodated questions? Run them on different colors of paper. Students select airplanes of their designated color to continue.

Appropriate for

- Traditional worksheets of any kind
- Essay questions
- Multistep problems
- Evaluating student work
- Vocabulary lists to define
- Open-ended or objective question types

Have you tried Paper Airplanes? Share on Twitter using #WorksheetBusters and #PaperAirplanes.

Musical Desks

The Gist: Students move around the room similar to the classic party game to complete the problems on a worksheet.

Why Do It: Playing Musical Desks gets students up and moving, narrows down how many problems they have to do, increases engagement and motivation, and brings some novelty to the school day. Musical Desks requires no special materials or preparation. This activity taps into students' love of music and dance moves, but the engagement isn't just in the movement. You'll find students work diligently when seated because they know they have an appropriate outlet for movement.

Materials

- Worksheet

Set Up

1. Cut a worksheet with numbered items into several slices, one item per slice.
2. Place one problem on each desk. If there are more items than desks, leave some out. If there are more desks than items, duplicate some items.
3. The game may be played with virtually any desk arrangement, or desks may be moved into a large circle.

To Play

1. Have students put their name on a piece of paper and number it according to however many items you have, starting with one.
2. Describe the correct flow of traffic through your desk arrangement if desks are not in a circle. Practice.
3. Play music and have the students boogie around the desks. When the music stops, they sit at the nearest desk and do that problem on their paper.
4. When they're ready, restart the music and repeat. Students should not repeat desks, so they need to go to a different vacant desk each time.
5. Play the game through your desired time or until you feel enough worksheet items were covered.

Caution and Tips

- Be very clear as to how students may move through your room. Unless you fully embrace classroom parkour, it might also be a good idea to remind students how you expect them to claim and then sit in a desk. Just take my word for it. You often don't *think* you have to stipulate such things, but you might want to.

- Be prepared with a couple printed copies of the worksheet in case any students choose not to comply with your expectations.
- Preview your music selection. This may not be the best time to take requests unless you're *very* familiar with the lyrics. Murphy's Law of Teaching says the moment an inappropriate word blares from your speakers will be the moment your administrator walks in for an unscheduled observation.

Variations

- Desks may be numbered (using sticky notes, numbered cards, dry erase, or overhead markers, etc.) and students carry around individual copies of the worksheet, then do the number they sit at instead of the method described above. This takes the least amount of prep work for the teacher, but I've found that when students physically touch a worksheet, their buy-in dips a bit. Few students get excited when handed a worksheet. Answering on their own paper or on papers left on the desks feels less like a worksheet.
- You can put a different problem or worksheet on each desk and have students work directly on that page, which stays on the desk. With this set up, students do different work each time they move (or cycle back to a problem they started earlier) and evaluate the work of others. This can lead to really valuable classroom conversation later, as students discuss what they noticed as they evaluated others and as they considered the feedback they received.
- If answering on paper left on the desks, students should initial the paper beside their own responses.
- If students are writing answers on paper left on the desks, they will encounter questions that have already been answered. Consider the list of metacognitive thought prompts listed below to help students extend their understanding. I like to have students answer the question on the first round and then defend or argue it on the second. I then display a different metacognitive thought prompt for each subsequent round. This gives students a bit more guidance on how to explain and extend their thinking.

- Musical Desks is also a great way to do trade-to-grade! Students can leave their assignment on their desks, walk until the music stops, and grade the paper at that desk. For open-ended items, students can rotate multiple times, leaving constructive feedback each time.
- You can do writing prompts or essay questions this way too. Start a prompt at one desk and leave it, then continue the writing at the next desk and repeat.

Differentiation Ideas

- Need varied, leveled, scaffolded, adapted, or accommodated questions? Run them on different colored paper. Students select desks of their designated color to continue.

Appropriate for

- Traditional worksheets of any kind
- Essay questions
- Multistep problems
- Evaluating student work
- Vocabulary lists to define
- Open-ended or objective question types

Metacognitive Thought Prompts

- What is your answer?
- How do you know your answer is correct?
- How do you know your answer is incorrect?
- Show your work, page number, or proof.
- What was your error?
- What is a strategy you used?
- What is a resource you used?
- What could you type into Google to find help for this problem?
- What do you wish you had asked or understood yesterday to be able to do this problem?
- What is an example that would have helped you with this problem?
- What vocabulary terms or skills are important to this problem?
- What did you find easy about the problem?
- What did you find difficult about the problem?
- How did your thinking about the problem change?
- What other homework item is this problem similar to? How are they similar?
- If you gave this problem a title, what would it be?
- How does this problem relate to something else you've learned?
- What questions about this content do you still have?
- What skills might someone need to be able to do this problem?
- What was a common error with this problem?
- What tip would you give someone who was just learning this content?
- How could you change this problem to make it easier, harder, or deeper?

- Why might you need this skill or knowledge outside of school?

Have you tried Musical Desks? Share using #WorksheetBusters and #MusicalDesks.

Speed Dating

The Gist: Students rotate with a question or answer until they find their perfect match.

Why Do It: This activity gets students talking about content, analyzing answer choices, and moving. Students have to evaluate whether their question or answer matches another and extend their thinking to consider what matches could be made.

Materials

- Questions from a worksheet (printed and cut apart)
- Answers (printed and cut apart)

Set Up

- Cut the worksheet and answer key apart.

To Play

1. Number students off as one and two. One group gets a question. The other gets an answer. Group students in partner pairs of one question person and one answer person (randomized rather than matching).
2. Set a time limit. Keep it tight—*just* long enough to think through the question and talk about the answer. The first "date" will be a bit longer than the others to give the students time to figure out the answer to their questions. You

can even use a bell the way many speed dating organizations do to signal time to rotate.

3. The partners compare the question and answer to determine if they are a match. If they are not a match, they work together to figure out what the correct answer could be. If students are rotating with a copy of the worksheet (see variations below), they can also try to figure out which question matches the other student's answer.
4. Ones or twos will rotate, then repeat step three. See variations below for ways to continue and end the activity. The most basic is that students continue rotating, even after they've found their match, to get needed information from other partners to complete their worksheet. Remember to keep "date" times tight.

Caution and Tips

- Some students are very comfortable with the dating idea of this activity, and you can play it up with themes, like "Single and Looking," "Hot Date," etc. However, these themes can make some students uncomfortable. Respect their dignity by being sensitive with how much you play up the dating scenario.
- If you have uneven numbers, you can serve as the missing player and use that rotation to interview the students about how they're doing so far.

Variations

- Give each student a copy of the worksheet (or have them number a piece of paper) to be completed as they rotate.
- Optionally, when a student finds their "perfect match," they exit the game and complete the rest of the worksheet with their new partner.

- You can mix up the questions and answers from time to time, so students have a different role and have to seek new matches.
- Play continues until each student has found their match, the assignment is completed, or until the class has reached the end of the designated play time.

Differentiation Ideas

- Need varied, leveled, scaffolded, adapted, or accommodated questions? Run them on different colors of paper. Students partner with those using the same color.

Appropriate for

- Traditional worksheets of any kind
- Vocabulary terms and definitions
- Objective question types

Have you tried Speed Dating? Share using #WorksheetBusters and #SpeedDating.

Q and A

The Gist: Each student gets both a question and an answer. Students form chains, matching questions to answers, similar to "I have, who has" games.

Why Do It: Playing Question and Answer gets students up and moving, interacting, and communicating to match questions to answers. Each student is initially responsible for just two questions but will eventually work through more. No special materials required!

Materials

- A worksheet and an answer key

Set Up

- Cut apart a worksheet and answer key. Keep a copy of the answer key for yourself.

To Play

1. Distribute one question and one answer to each student.
2. Give students a moment to solve their questions.
3. On your signal, students try to find the person with their answer. One student's matching answer will belong to a student whose question matches someone else, and so on.

TIP: Instruct students to hold the question in their left hand and the answer in their right. This will facilitate arranging matches into chains. Students stand side-by-side with their matching person and continue to gather matching people on either side.

4. Students work to form the longest chain possible. In order for their chain to count, all answers must be correct. Students should work together to check all questions. When they believe their chain is complete and correct, they sit down to signal to you that they're ready to be checked.
5. Check the matches using your key. The longest correct chain wins!
6. Redistribute questions and answers and repeat.

Caution and Tips

- Some students will "match" two different chains as chains arrange themselves. They must decide which they go to or encourage the chains to combine.

- Students often try to trade slips until they're holding a match. Practice a round really emphasizing holding on to their own slips and physically moving to match the people next to them, instead of trying to have matching slips in their own hands. The objective isn't to *hold* a match but to form a chain of matches side-by-side.
- If students cannot behave according to your expectations during the activity, they can be sent back to their desk to complete the entire worksheet on their own.
- Organization matters. Each question in play needs to have a matching answer, so assemble and distribute questions and answers carefully. At the end of your final round, gather and store questions and answers in matching pairs to make it easier to prepare for your next class.

Variations

- If the whole class can form one correct chain, everyone wins! Consider awarding them a special bonus.
- You can provide individual copies of the worksheet to students and have them record answers from their groups. Remind them they are responsible for deciding if those answers are correct or not and will be responsible for their grades.
- You can use a class roster to keep track of individual points for cumulative winners or just acknowledge winning groups for each round.
- To play with vocabulary, give each student a term and a definition and instruct them to form chains of matches.

Differentiation Ideas

- You can pre-select the problems students receive to ensure they are solving appropriate problems. The fact that students will be forming teams and communicating to check answers together provides built-in support.

Appropriate for

- Worksheets with objective right or wrong answers
- Vocabulary

Have you tried Q and A? Share using #WorksheetBusters and #QandA.

Sorting Activities

The Gist: Students analyze worksheet items and the relationships between them to determine what categories they can group them into.

Why Do It: Rather than getting students to answer questions on yet another worksheet, this activity makes students actually *think* about the content in front of them. This activity is more about making connections with the content. It also lets them physically manipulate worksheet items. This is applicable to any content.

Materials

- A worksheet

Set Up

- Print and cut apart the worksheet problems for each group.

To Play

1. Group students in partnerships or small groups of three.
2. Give each group the cut-apart worksheet. Tell them to consider those items and then sort them however they see

fit. If you feel it's appropriate, they may even use their textbook or other resources to help them learn more about each item. Students will have to consider what each item means, how it's used, and how the problems are related to one another to be able to sort them. You could have categories in mind—like parts of speech, types of rocks, positive vs. negative numbers, etc.—or you can just see what the students come up with.

3. When a student group feels their items are sorted, they give each category a title or description.
4. Next, students explain, either in person or in writing, how they grouped the problems and determined those categories.
5. If you intend for students to determine specific categories (e.g., parts of speech, types of rocks, etc.), provide feedback and probing questions to help them see these connections.

If categories are more open-ended, tell groups to share what they came up with.

Caution and Tips

- Students might try sorting items, like "These are short" or "I know these and don't know these." Although that's not where we want them to finish, use it as a place to start. Say things like, "Okay, if you don't know these problems, here's a resource you can use. Find out more about them and refine your groups."
- Be present as groups work. If you notice one partner carrying more of the load than another, ask questions of the partner who is working less to gauge his or her understanding. If needed, you can even give them a specific role, like looking up each word in the text or sorting half the items.

Variations

- Instead of using a worksheet, you can use a vocabulary list, a list of facts, etc. Students can sort the terms and ideas into categories.
- You can pick items that should organize into certain categories (e.g., parts of speech, types of rocks, etc.) or just see what students come up with as they extend their understanding.
- Students can take a gallery walk to look at how other groups have categorized their items.

Differentiation Ideas

- Consider giving some groups the intended category titles (though I recommend first seeing what they come up with on their own).

Appropriate for

- Worksheets
- Vocabulary lists
- Lists of facts from your content
- Word lists related to your content

Have you tried Sorting Activities? Share using #WorksheetBusters and #SortingActivities.

Interval Races

The Gist: Students compete in a relay to complete a worksheet against an unpredictable interval timer.

Why Do It: The unpredictable nature of the interval timer keeps students on their toes and interest high. The only materials you need are a worksheet and the timer! This activity was born out of an idea to use sand timers in a worksheet relay. There was only one problem: I couldn't find the sand timers. A slightly panicked Google search led me to a free online timer, so I quickly whipped together a series of random time intervals, crossed my fingers, and launched the activity. It was a smashing success! The anticipation of never knowing when that timer is going off keeps the energy high!

Materials

- One copy of the worksheet for each group
- Use an online interval timer set to random lengths of time (I like the one found at online-stopwatch.com/interval-timer or simply Google "free online interval timers."). I have mine set in durations of several seconds to a couple minutes in length.

Set Up

- The timer should be pulled up with the sound on, but don't display the timer to the students. You don't want them to know when it's going to go off!
- Arrange the class in teams and set them up for a relay with one player seated at the desk and the others lined up behind. I recommend teams of three.

To Play

1. Distribute one copy of the worksheet to each team, face down.
2. Go over the rules:
    - Only the player seated at the desk may work the problems.
    - The teammates cannot help.

- When the timer sounds, the next player takes the seat and resumes working.
- Players may change answers, skip around, etc.

NOTE: Because the timer will sound soon, players will not feel too much pressure if they're unsure. Furthermore, waiting players won't get too antsy or off-task. The unpredictable timer will keep anticipation high!

3. Start the timer and say "go." Players switch at the sound and continue until a team believes they have completed the worksheet, and all answers are correct.
4. When a team believes they are done, they all put their hands up. Pause the timer and have other teams turn their papers over and put their pencils down. Check that team's work. The moment you find a mistake, resume the timer and let other teams continue while you finish checking that "done" team. This gives teams incentive to be sure they're correct before putting their hands up, avoiding random answers.
5. Continue until a team has all answers correct or you call time, at which point the winner is the team with the most correct answers.

Caution and Tips

- Observe carefully while teams work to keep an eye on who seems to be getting the content and who isn't. This activity does not provide you with solid data to this nature and is intended for practice rather than data to drive instruction.
- Although I avoid activities where students are waiting with nothing to do, I've found the unpredictable timer keeps them waiting with bated breath, and I have not had much trouble with off-task students. However, keep

groups small to minimize wait time. Three has been the magic number for me.

Variations

- Want to use open-ended questions? Instead of a worksheet relay, put discussion questions on each desk with notebook paper. Have students start at a desk and write an answer until the timer goes off and then rotate to the next desk, continuing that problem until the timer sounds. This is similar to Musical Desks, but students rotate to the very next desk when the timer sounds.

Differentiation Ideas

- Need varied, leveled, scaffolded, adapted, or accommodated questions? Group students by need and supply each group with the assignment that best meets their needs. The whole class doesn't have to be doing the same worksheet!

Appropriate for

- Worksheets with objective answers
- Multistep problems with objective answers
- Open-ended questions if using the variation above

Have you tried Interval Races? Share using #WorksheetBusters and #IntervalRaces.

Chapter 5

LOW PREP, LOW MATERIALS

Hungry Hippos

The Gist: Students gather balls to determine which problems they work on.

Why Do It: Remember when the videos of people playing a giant, human-sized version of Hungry Hippos went viral around social media a few years ago? If you haven't seen the videos, check out this one from Blaine Christenson: bit.ly/HungryHipposVideo. I saw the videos and wondered how I could bring that energy and fun into my classroom. Thus, the Worksheet Buster Hungry Hippos was born. (Well, minus the gym dollies. I'm terrified of those. People lose fingers!) Playing Hungry Hippos gets students up and moving in a very novel, hands-on way. This activity can also give them an opportunity to work collaboratively in small groups.

Materials

- Ball pit balls (one per worksheet item or one per student)
- Permanent marker

Directions to Make

- Use a permanent marker to write one number (typically one through thirty) on each ball.

Set Up

- Place the balls in the middle of your floor.

To Play

1. Give every student a worksheet or a digital copy.
2. Divide students into equal teams and have team members sit together near the edge of the playing space.
3. At your signal, one player from each team rushes to the pile of balls and gathers enough for each member of the team to have one. (If teams are unequal, teams should gather an equal number of balls.) The player returns to their team and distributes the balls.
4. Everyone answers their question on their own worksheet and reports their answer to the player who gathered the balls. That person records their team's answers on their own worksheet and brings it to the teacher to check.
5. The teacher marks answers right or wrong. The team gets one point for each correct answer.
6. Repeat with each player taking a turn gathering balls and recording answers.
7. You can create a rule that teams can't repeat problems they've already done, which keeps the game challenging, as they'll have to swap balls with other teams or the ball pile. Or they may repeat problems, which means their

responsibility may be rewarded if they've kept good track of their work.

8. The game ends when every player has had a turn or when you reach the end of the desired playing time.
9. The team with the most points wins.

*Some of you have already lost your mind every time you read the word "balls." Don't even try to deny it. Just see below.

Caution and Tips

- If teaching middle or high school students, be prepared for giggling every time you say the word *balls*. Have a lighthearted conversation about it and embrace the laughter. I recommend heretofore renaming balls "learning spheres." The conversation goes something like this . . .

Teacher (holding up a ball): "This is a ball."
Students (looking at each other to decide if it's okay to laugh): *snickering*
Teacher: "Now, this ball is a valuable learning tool."
Students: *snickering*
Teacher: "And because this ball is a valuable learning tool, it will now be known as a 'learning sphere.' Everyone, what is this?"
Students: "A learning sphere!"

- Set clear expectations about how students may approach the ball/learning sphere pile (e.g., whether or not running is allowed, not to crash into people, etc.), so you don't have a hands-on demonstration in traumatic brain injury via concussion. I recommend tiptoeing, crab walking, grapevining, etc.
- Be clear how the balls are to be managed during turns. If it will drive you crazy for them to be bounced, tossed, rolled, squished, or otherwise manipulated, set those boundaries before the game starts. Really, this has more to do with your tolerance level than theirs. Don't set them up to drive you bonkers!
- If those balls are going to drive you crazy, go around and collect them once students know which problems they're doing.
- If students cannot behave according to your expectations during the activity, they can be sent back to their desks to complete the entire worksheet on their own.
- Contain the balls somehow. I borrow a hula-hoop from the PE teacher, but the bag the balls originally came in works too!

Variations

- Tape questions or content directly to the balls. If the relay game version sounds too complicated, this variation is the simplest to implement. Students select a ball and answer that question, either on their own paper or through discussion.
- The game may be played individually instead of on teams. More students will be running at each other, though, so be prepared.
- The game can be played in reverse, where the problems gathered are the ones they *don't* have to do.
- To play with vocabulary, write or tape definitions on the balls. Students can then answer with the matching terms (or vice versa).
- Hungry Hippos can easily be used for class discussion. Simply tape a discussion question on each ball. Students select a ball and then gather in small groups (such as by color or number) to discuss their questions together.
- My favorite variation: Station different problems or worksheets around the room and assign different ball numbers to each page. For example, if I had ten worksheets around the room, each worksheet would have three sphere numbers. Every student draws a ball and goes to the corresponding problem. Some students may be in a group while others may be working alone. Give them a few minutes, then redraw. This lets students work in many different arrangements and on many different problems. Students going to a page after another group has already started it need to evaluate whether or not they agree with the work that's started and continue.
- You can play Hot Potato with these balls. The students stand in a circle facing inward, each with a ball. They pass

the balls around the circle, behind their backs, while you play music. When the music stops, they do the problem associated with the ball they're holding.

- Students can be required to get any answers they didn't have from other students at the conclusion of the game. This gets them to interact and discuss their thinking together.
- See the Lecture Buster variation of Hungry Hippos (see page 131).

Differentiation Ideas

- Hungry Hippos is easy to differentiate for a variety of student learning needs. Make sure certain colors correspond to specific problems and have select students draw only that color. You can arrange that specification secretly with individual students or group students by color and have each team draw only that color. The assignment is differentiated then without making "levels" obvious to the students. They'll just think that's the blue team! You can even have a "rainbow team" that is allowed to draw any color.

Appropriate for

- Worksheets
- Open-ended questions
- Vocabulary

Have you tried Hungry Hippos? Share using #WorksheetBusters and #HungryHippos.

Go on Six

The Gist: Have you ever played the party game where candy, money, and other treats are wrapped up in a ball of cellophane?

This Worksheet Buster brings that same fun and energy to any worksheet! Students race to finish their worksheets before someone rolls a six and takes over.

Why Do It: The unpredictable nature of the rolls keeps this activity competitive and highly engaging. All you need is a worksheet and some dice!

Materials

- One copy of the worksheet for each student
- One die for every three or four students

Set Up

- Arrange students into teams of three or four.
- Have one copy of the worksheet ready for each student, one die for each team, and one pencil for each team.

To Play

1. Distribute a copy of the worksheet to each player, face down.
2. Go over the rules: One player starts with the pencil and will be the first to work on the worksheet. The student to the right gets the die. On "Go!" the student with the pencil begins the worksheet while the student with the die starts rolling. The other player(s) can read the worksheet and think of answers but cannot write yet.
3. When the player with the die rolls a six, he or she takes the pencil from the original player, and the die passes to the right. Repeat play with these players performing their new roles.
4. Continue until someone believes he or she is done. When a player believes he or she is done, all other players turn their papers over while you check that player's work. If you

find a mistake, he or she may resume play. Alternatively, you may call "Time!" and check whatever they've finished.

Caution and Tips

- Keep teams small so that no player is idle for very long.
- Allowing students to look at their worksheets between turns provides opportunity to keep thinking and planning and keeps them engaged on content.

Variations

- Teams can compete to have the most questions correct.
- Multiple dice could be going at one time in each team to keep play unpredictable.
- This activity can be used for essay-style questions or multistep problems. Additionally, one essay or long problem could be worked on by the whole group, with the problem passing from person to person, instead of each person having his or her own.
- This game can be played with Left, Right, Center dice. To play this variation, students are put into teams of four. The player working first works one problem, then rolls the die to determine if play moves to the left, right, or center (across). Again, this can be done with individual worksheets or one per team.

Differentiation Ideas

- Student groups can complete different worksheets. They can be grouped so that every player in a group has the same version of the worksheet, or groups can be mixed. The routine works just as well, even if students are working on different worksheets at the same time.

Appropriate for

- Worksheets with objective right or wrong answers

Have you tried Go on Six? Share using #WorksheetBusters and #GoonSix.

Strike a Pose

The Gist: Students respond to multiple-choice questions by striking the corresponding pose.

Why Do It: Getting students up and out of their desks and physically responding to your questions encourages participation and increases the fun of any lesson. You can also quickly and easily see both who's got it and who doesn't.

Materials

- ABCD Pose Images (Make your own or use mine, available at teachbeyondthedesk.com/strike-a-pose.)
- Multiple-choice questions

Set Up

- Select or create a set of multiple-choice questions.
- Save the ABCD Pose Images to display with your questions. (These can be projected, embedded in a slideshow, etc.)

To Play

1. Assign multiple-choice questions.
2. Display the pose pictures.
3. Students strike the pose that corresponds with their answer.
4. Laugh and giggle. Look around to get an idea of who's got it and who doesn't.
5. Show the correct answer.
6. Repeat.

Caution and Tips

- Give clear expectations for pose-striking behavior (e.g., hands and bodies must be kept to self, etc.). Note that the karate pose is not permission to kick your neighbor in the jaw.
- Have the students spread out a bit.
- Students will look at one another to try to decide which pose is correct. That's okay. This is not meant to be an individual assessment, and you can still notice who is posing with confidence and who's a bit more reluctant.

Variations

- Make your own pose cards, using pictures of the students and their own poses.
- This can be integrated with classroom yoga for a brain break that doesn't interrupt your lesson.

Adaptations for Students with Special Physical Needs

- Students who cannot strike the pose can use just the arm position, or you can print the pose pictures as cards for them to hold up.

Appropriate for

- Multiple-choice questions

Have you tried Strike a Pose? Share using #WorksheetBusters and #StrikeaPose.

Heads-Up Seven-Up

The Gist: This twist on the classic game gets students up and moving to match questions to answers.

Why Do It: We all know this classic classroom game. It's our go-to when the assembly lets out early, leaving us with fifteen minutes to fill before dismissal. But it isn't very academic, is it? I sought to change that, resulting in this engaging Worksheet Buster. Heads-Up Seven-Up gets students up and moving around, encourages them to think more critically about the content, increases engagement and motivation, and generally breaks up the monotony of a regular school day.

Materials

- Plastic page protector sleeves (one per student)
- Worksheet questions and answers (printed one per page or written on the plastic sleeves)
- String or yarn

Set Up

1. Write or print worksheet questions and answers individually (one per page).

NOTE: Number the problems to make it easier to stay organized and check matches.

2. Tie an 18- to 24-inch length of string or yarn through the top and bottom holes of the page protectors to make a giant necklace-like sign.
3. Have a copy of the answer key ready for you to use to check answers.

To Play

1. Slip the answers into page protector sleeves.
2. Match up questions and answers, so you can make sure every question in play has an answer in play. Pick seven questions to be used by the "up" students (those who stand and tap to select a student) to start with and then select an answer for each of the seated students (being sure to include the answers that match the questions selected for the "up" students).
3. Give each seated student an answer to wear, so the answer lays on his or her back. Do not let seated students see what answer they're wearing. Give each "up" student a question to wear, so it hangs in the front.
4. "Up" students stand at the front of the room, displaying their questions. All students, "up" and seated, work out the problems the "up" students are wearing. Students can work them out on their own copy of the worksheet, on notebook paper, or on whiteboards.
5. Seated students lay their heads down and hide their eyes. "Up" students walk around till they find the student with their answer (displayed on the backs of seated students).

"Up" students tap the students with their answers, and tapped students raise their hands (or put a thumb up).

6. When all answers are found, "up" students return to the front of the room, seated students pick their heads up, and tapped students stand up.
7. Seated and tapped students turn their answer signs around to the front.
8. One by one, tapped students say who they think tapped them (based on whose question their answer matches). Correctly tapped students trade places with their "up" match.
9. Collect the answer signs and redistribute (to mix them up). Distribute new questions to the new "up" students and make sure seated students all have different answers.

HINT: Organization matters. As new questions are rotated in, make sure the matching answers are also brought into play.

10. Repeat steps five through nine until end of play time.

Caution and Tips

- You can distribute copies of the worksheet and have students fill in answers as players guess their matches each round. This is not essential but may hold students accountable to being on task.
- Organization is pretty important. Keep questions and matching answers organized together as you rotate problems in and out of play to ensure every "up" question has a matching answer in play. There will be more answers in play than questions, meaning most seated students do not have a matching question in play. That's fine—it's just like having four answer choices for one test question. Rotating answers and bringing new questions in each round keeps play fair and gives more students an opportunity to be picked.
- One potential challenge to be aware of is that students who are not picked each round may be tempted to "check out" as picked students name their matches. To keep all students engaged, consider having every student write the answer on a whiteboard and hold it up, give evidence to prove the matches, etc.
- Plan what to do if a student is wrong about who picked them. You can allow another student to "steal" by proving they know the right answer. Or you can allow that "up" student to remain "up" for another round.
- If students cannot behave according to your expectations during the activity, they can be sent back to their desks to complete the entire worksheet on their own.

Variations

- The same process can be used with terms and definitions.

- Page protector sleeves work as a dry-erase surface. You can slip blank paper in and write on the plastic instead of printing questions and answers.

Differentiation Ideas

- If you're concerned about putting certain students on the spot to try and name who picked them in front of the rest of the class, you can check their work before the round starts and provide assistance as needed, especially if you notice they are wearing an answer that will be "picked" that round.

Appropriate for

- Questions with objective right or wrong answers
- Vocabulary

Have you tried Heads-Up Seven-Up? Share using #WorksheetBusters and #HeadsUpSevenUp.

Poker

The Gist: Students draw a card to determine which problem they do, then find students whose cards make the designated hand.

Why Do It: Playing this version of Poker requires students to collaborate and cooperate as they work together to solve problems.

Materials

- Playing cards

Set Up

1. Pull out the face cards (except the Ace) and set them aside. These are not needed.

2. Choose ten problems from your worksheet and number them.

To Play

1. Make sure the worksheet is narrowed down and renumbered accordingly. Copy and distribute the worksheet.
2. Students write their names on the board to keep score, or the teacher records the score on a copy of the class roster.
3. Deal one card to each student. Students complete that problem.
4. When everyone is ready, call out a hand, like four of a kind, straight flush, or full house.

NOTE: Four of a kind is the simplest to start with.

5. Students scramble to find people with corresponding cards to form that hand. Students who do not find a hand to join should make a group together (like the "chance" in Yahtzee).
6. Once grouped, students should work together to make sure they agree on their team members' answers. Students record those answers on their own worksheets so that, by the end of the round, their original problem *and* all group members' problems are solved on their own copies of the worksheet.
7. When ready, they go to the teacher to have their answers checked. If all members have the correct answers, each member scores one point for that hand. If even one member is incorrect, the team does not receive any points. All players record their own number of points earned for each round.
8. Disband groups, deal cards again, and repeat as long as desired.
9. Players with the highest final scores win.

Caution and Tips

- If you call four of a kind, this gives struggling students a chance to check their answer against those of three other people. This is also an easy hand for inexperienced card players to understand.
- Students who do not find a hand to join may form a larger group. This gives them a greater challenge to make sure *every* member of the group is correct.
- Have examples of the hands ready to show the students, so those with little card-playing experience understand.
- Be prepared with a couple printed copies of the worksheet, in case any students choose not to comply with your expectations.

Variations

- Do not call out a hand. Instead, allow students to group themselves. Give points according to highest hand point value (according to standard Poker rules).
- Play with *UNO* cards and have students group by color or number. Players with no match would be out for the round.
- Distribute cards but don't ask students to solve that problem. Instead, have students form groups by making hands, then those groups work together to complete the worksheet in its entirety.

Differentiation Ideas

- Start with four of a kind to give students the opportunity to check their answers with other students.
- Allow students to keep the same card or problem for several hands.

Appropriate for

- Worksheets

Have you tried Poker? Share using
#WorksheetBusters and #Poker.

Grocery List

The Gist: Students find problems that match a list of descriptors.

Why Do It: Answering questions on a worksheet provides some practice, sure, but drive it deeper by expecting students to analyze their answers and the questions while they move around the room.

Materials

- Worksheet
- List of descriptors (mixed up to create multiple versions)

NOTE: Lists do not have to include every problem.

Set Up

1. Cut apart the worksheet and post individual questions around the room.
2. Prepare and print multiple versions of the "grocery list" (i.e., a list of descriptors or attributes your students are looking for in the worksheet problems or answers. For example, "has a negative answer," "the opposite of a protagonist," "a geographic feature north of Mexico," "solved by addition," "answer is a comma splice," etc.).
3. Create an answer key for each list, indicating which problem(s) work(s) for each item on the list.

NOTE: This does take a bit more prep work than many Worksheet Busters, but the depth of learning is totally worth it.

Example grocery lists, both designed for the same equations worksheet:

Name______________________	Name______________________
Record one PROBLEM that meets the description. 1) Solved by division. 2) Answer is 8. 3) Answer is 11. 4) Solved by addition. 5) Requires you to write an addition equation.	Record one PROBLEM that meets the description. 1) Solved by multiplication. 2) Answer is 9. 3) Answer is 39. 4) Solved by subtraction. 5) Requires you to write an addition equation.

To Play

1. Give each student a grocery list.
2. Send them around the room to look at and solve the problems you've posted. When they find a problem that matches what they're looking for, they record that problem number next to the item on their grocery list.

NOTE: It is possible that more than one problem works for an item on the grocery list. That's okay!

3. Either collect and grade the lists or have students meet in groups to discuss. To simplify this process, have students with the same list meet together. You can label lists as A, B, C, etc., or by color.

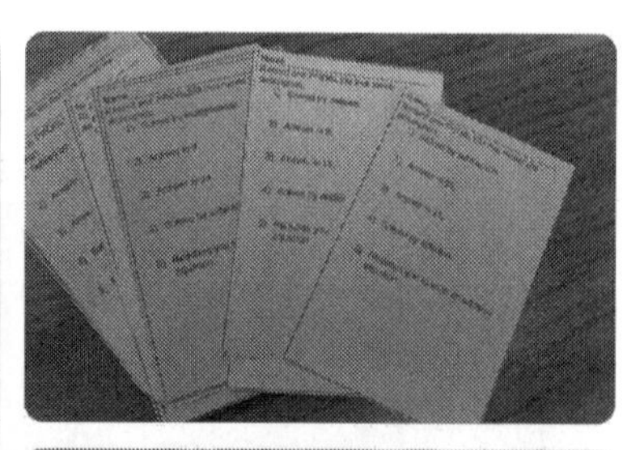

Caution and Tips

- Consider a silence rule, so students work independently until it's time to meet and discuss.
- Be prepared with something to do for students who finish early or challenge them to find as many problems as possible for each item on their lists.
- Explore varying the DOK of items on your grocery list. Regardless of the DOK of the worksheet itself, you can increase or decrease the depth with how you word your list. See examples.
- Unless you are collecting the lists prior to discussion, this activity will not provide solid data about how individual students are doing on the content. This activity is effective

for practice toward mastery but not as an assessment *unless* you collect the lists without discussing.

Variations

- If students seem to be guessing which problems match the items on their list, give them a few minutes to solve the worksheet on their own before sending them around the room to "shop" for problems.
- Make it competitive by asking students to find as many problems that match each descriptor as possible. Deduct points for problems they include that don't match to discourage random guessing.
- Have students write grocery lists and answer keys and then use those lists for the activity. They can work in groups to make the list and then challenge another group to complete their list.
- Instead of posting worksheet problems, post student essay answers (numbered for identification purposes). Make a list of descriptors, like "includes a clear thesis statement," "lacks a conclusion," "includes only one piece of evidence," etc. Out of respect for students, I recommend you remove students' names from work samples before posting.
- Post articles on your content topic, use questions as grocery list items, and have students walk around to find the answers in the articles or analyze the articles for how effectively they present their arguments, etc.

Differentiation Ideas

- Assign lists appropriate for student needs, such as higher or lower DOK, scaffolded supports, targeting specific skills, etc.

- When students meet with other students who had the same grocery list, they'll be able to check their answers, provide support, and develop confidence.

Appropriate for

- Worksheets
- Student work samples
- Essay responses
- Articles and other text

Have you tried Grocery List? Share using #WorksheetBusters and #GroceryList.

Block Tower

The Gist: Students get a block with an answer on it and try to stack them in order to match the assignment.

Why Do It: Blocks are fun! And working together on a single class tower means every student's contribution counts.

Materials

- Basic Mega Bloks® (the big kind designed for preschoolers), one for each problem or student
- An assignment

Set Up

1. Print or copy the answer key, cut it apart (making sure to cut off the numbers), and tape one answer to each block.
2. Optional: Stack the blocks in order, with the first answer at the top on down to the last, and take a picture to help you check each tower during play. Alternately, you can just use the worksheet answer key.

To Play

1. Distribute a copy of the worksheet to each student.
2. Give each student a block or let them each draw one block from the bag.
3. Allow time for students to work problems on the assignment to find which problem number their answer block goes with. This requires students to use some good deductive reasoning to narrow down which problems their answer could match. Chances are they'll work several problems until they find the one that matches their answer.
4. Students work together to stack the blocks in order, the answer to number one at the top on down to the last on the bottom. Building in this order means students have to work together to keep the tower up, facilitating greater buy-in from students who have already had their turn. Students navigate disagreements to settle on a "correct" answer.
5. You check their tower. If they are wrong, redistribute blocks and try again. If it is totally correct, either play again by redistributing the blocks or end the game.

Caution and Tips

- Some students are better leaders than others. Try to allow them to reach a consensus without your intervention but be ready to step in if any students are being belittled or marginalized.
- If a class is particularly large or easily gets off-task once their part is done, consider one of the variations below.
- If you have more students than questions and answers, students can work as partners.

Variations

- Make two or three sets and divide the class into smaller groups.
- Groups can race to see who can build their tower first.
- If using smaller groups, you can give each student multiple blocks to match or use smaller problem sets.
- If using smaller problem sets, you can use different assignments for each group and even rotate students through the sets after successfully building each tower.
- Consider a silent build—students may not talk as they arrange the answer blocks in order.
- Use this activity to match vocabulary to definitions. Give each student a term to match to a numbered list of definitions or vice versa.

Differentiation Ideas

- Use the colors of blocks to differentiate, assigning content of different difficulty levels or question types to appropriate students.

Appropriate for

- Worksheets with objective right or wrong answers
- Vocabulary

Have you tried Block Tower? Share using #WorksheetBusters and #BlockTower.

Sock Hop

The Gist: Students match answers to questions by wearing a giant sock over their shoe.

Why Do It: The silly novelty of this activity easily engages most students, but the academic effort needed to work backward from an answer to the matching question means deep learning is still taking place.

Materials

- Very large men's athletic socks, thirty total (fifteen pairs)
- A permanent marker
- An assignment

Set Up

1. Using a permanent marker, number each sock, one through thirty, large and clear.
2. Print the answer key and cut it apart to separate each answer. Make sure you cut off the numbers.
3. Copy the worksheet for each student.
4. Pile the socks in the middle of the floor.

To Play

1. Distribute a copy of the worksheet to each student.
2. Give each student an answer.
3. Allow time for students to work problems from the assignment to find which question their answer matches.
4. At your signal, students go to the sock pile and find the sock with the number representing the problem their answer matches.
5. To claim their number, students put that sock over their shoe and hop back to their seat holding the socked foot up.
6. If a student feels someone else claimed his or her sock, he or she must work together to figure it out.
7. Play continues until all matches are made. Redistribute and repeat. (See variations below!) Students will have worked most, if not all, of the worksheet by the end of play.

10

Caution and Tips

- Inevitably, someone will take a sock that should match someone else's answer. If students just grab a random sock in an effort to be "done," it will throw off everyone else's matches. I sometimes allow that to happen for a round, then we discuss how well that worked and how we might make it smoother. If students can't find their match in the pile, they can stand by the student who claimed it. The class can then discuss the disagreement to determine what the correct match should be.
- Designate a special way that students must go to the pile each time to avoid football-like collisions. For example, students could waddle like a duck, tiptoe, etc.
- If you have more students than assignment items, students can work as a pair. Only one of them would go to the sock pile and go back and put the sock on his or her partner's foot.
- The socks will get looser and easier to use the more you play.

Variations

- Turn this into a relay race! Group students into teams after distributing answers. They sit or stand in a line like a traditional relay race. The first player goes to the pile to claim his or her sock and hops back. The next player cannot start until the sock is actually on the shoe enough to stay on, and the player has hopped past them. The first team done (with correct matches) wins.
- Play as a whole group against your own time. Time the first round, then redistribute and play again to beat the previous time.

- Keep points—students who correctly match their answers and problems get a point. (But, honestly, timing the rounds is a bit easier and creates a we're-all-in-this-together mentality.)
- Play with a vocabulary list by numbering a list of terms and distributing definitions (or vice versa).

Differentiation Ideas

- You can be intentional about what answers you distribute to students.
- Additionally, you can narrow down which problems a student considers. Since you know what problem they match, you can tell them which column, row, etc., on the worksheet to try.
- If you anticipate a student may struggle, be ready to preserve his or her dignity if he or she claims a sock that should go to someone else. He or she isn't likely to be the only student to make a mistake, and a classroom culture that values learning necessitates making mistakes because mistakes are a part of learning. But be ready and be present.

Appropriate for

- Worksheets with objective right or wrong answers
- Vocabulary

Have you tried Sock Hop? Share using #WorksheetBusters and #SockHop.

Chapter 6

More Prep, More Materials (But Still Worth It!)

Giant Bull's-Eye

Adapted from the Bull's-Eye Answers strategy created by educational consultant Kristina Smekens.

The Gist: This hands-on activity provides a concrete way for students to evaluate and sort potential answer choices.

The outermost ring of the bull's-eye is for answer choices that are far from correct. They may be factually incorrect, untrue, or otherwise obviously not correct.

The next ring is for answer choices that are true or factually correct but don't answer the question being asked.

The next ring is for answers that seem correct, both factually and in the context of the question. We gather answers we think may be right for consideration as we look for the *best* answer.

Then we compare those options and isolate the one (or more in select-all situations) that are the *best fit* for the question.

Why Do It: Regardless of how we feel about standardized testing, the reality is we owe our students exposure to, practice with, and strategies for the question formats they're likely to see. This activity gets students up and moving to narrow answer choices and select the "bull's-eye answer." And this strategy certainly isn't limited to test prep! Use it for any multiple-choice or select-all question!

Materials

- Large sheet of heavy-weight plastic sheeting (I used a 10 ft. x 10 ft. 4 mil sheet.)
- Duct tape (optional: four different colors to differentiate the rings more)
- String
- Dry-erase marker
- ABCD cards printed in a different color for each group
- Multiple-choice questions

Directions to Make

The first time I did this, I used floor tape. It's a wonderful invention and one of my favorite teaching materials. My school's PE teacher has tons of it and gave me a roll. This is the same tape used to mark gym floors, so it sticks to the floor but leaves no adhesive residue behind. It's perfectly safe! I labeled each ring using masking tape on the floor tape.

But then I realized I'd have to make it all over again the next time I wanted to use it (or I'd just have to live with a giant bull's-eye in the middle of my floor—and if you've been paying attention, you know I use my floor a lot, so that's just not going to work).

Thus, I introduced one of my other favorite teaching materials: painter's plastic. Using a 10 ft. x 10 ft. sheet of plastic drop cloth (as seen in Giant Grid and Candy Land), I marked the rings. A piece of string tied to a dry-erase marker and taped in the center of the bull's-eye made my circles rounder than I could have managed free-hand. The plastic version makes this strategy reusable and easy to deploy. I keep it folded up in my cabinet. I can even bring it out on a whim when I realize it might help students.

To Play

1. Partner students and give each partnership a set of ABCD answer cards.
2. Take a moment to explicitly teach students how the bull's-eye works, as described above.
3. Assign a multiple-choice question. Partners discuss where each answer choice would belong on the bull's-eye.

NOTE: Remind them every ring may not be used for every question and that it is okay to have more than one answer choice in the same ring.

4. At your signal, one person from each partnership places their answer choices on the bull's-eye, face down to keep their choices secret.
5. When every group is ready, have a "big reveal" to see what each group chose. This gives you a great opportunity to discuss distractors, why choices were right or wrong, etc. You'll also have immediate feedback on how each group is doing, what concepts need further reteaching, etc.
6. You can keep score by awarding a point to each group that identified the correct answer.
7. Have students gather up their color of ABCD cards and repeat the process for the next question.

Caution and Tips

- I've found that partnerships work best for this activity. When I've tried groups of three or more, at least one person in each group tends to be more off-task for this activity.
- Classroom management tends to be easier with this activity. Although students get up and moving, the physical movement is really tame compared to a lot of Worksheet Busters.

Variations

- You can provide students a printed version of a bull's-eye to independently sort and record answer choices to provide accountability during the activity and to transition from this whole-group activity to an independent multiple-choice strategy.

- I like to do a few questions together using Giant Bull's-Eye and then assign a few for students to do independently, so I have more specific data on each student's mastery.
- The bull's-eye can also be used to sort text evidence and other concepts. If students have trouble selecting evidence from the text, this can directly support the concept in question. You can even put individual statements from the text on the index cards (print, cut, paste) and physically sort them.
- You can bring the target out and lay it down during independent testing. It serves as a visual reminder of how to think through these problems! But please clear this with your testing coordinator before using it for any standardized test—you know how stingy those rules are!
- If I'm going to invest the time to make something like this, I want to get a lot of bang for my buck and time! So this bull's-eye can be used for another Worksheet Buster called Curling. (Curious how you could use this bull's-eye with other homework assignments? See page 170.)

Differentiation Ideas

- Be mindful how you partner students. Thoughtful partnerships may be the only step you need to take to adequately support students of various learning needs.

Appropriate for

- Multiple-choice questions
- Multiple-select or select-all-that-apply questions
- Sorting and selecting supporting evidence

Have you tried Giant Bull's-Eye? Share using #WorksheetBusters and #GiantBullsEye.

Curling

The Gist: Teams aim a ball with their answer choice on the target to knock their opponents out of the rings and to try and win the most points. This idea uses the Giant Bull's-Eye and some balls—ahem, learning spheres—from Hungry Hippos. If you've been to my workshops before, you may have seen this idea presented as Shuffleboard. After thoughtful participation in my school's Winter-Olympics-themed version, I decided Curling is a better fit.

Why Do It: A little competition, balanced with collaboration with one's teammates, plus the fun of aiming anything at a target, makes this an engaging way to get students answering questions.

Materials

- Giant Bull's-Eye (see page 81)
- Ball pit balls (one for each team)
- Dry-erase markers (one for each team)
- Worksheet or question set

Directions to Make

- None if you've already made your bull's-eye. (Find more directions on page 81)

Set Up

- Push desks out of the way to clear floor space for the bull's-eye.
- Using dry-erase marker, number the space outside the rings 1, the outer-most ring 2, then 3, and so on until the center of the bull's-eye is worth 5 points.

LET
WRITING

To Play

1. Distribute one worksheet to each student or otherwise project or share questions for them to answer.
2. Divide students into teams.
3. Give each team one ball (I use a different color for each team, or since the balls are numbered from Hungry Hippos, each team could have a number).
4. Each team talks together to answer the first question.
5. One player from each team writes the answer on his or her ball using a dry erase marker.
6. Those players are the first to roll. They stand outside the target with their feet off the plastic. For the first round, all teams roll at the same time. Their feet cannot touch the plastic during their roll.
7. Teams score the points for the ring their ball landed in if their answer is correct. Correct answers that stopped outside the target get one point.
8. Teams work together again to answer the next question. The next player up writes the answer on the ball. For each subsequent round, players roll one at a time, starting with the team with the highest point total. Each subsequent team can try to knock other teams out of the rings. Starting with the highest-scoring team keeps the competition hot!
9. Check answers, add points, and continue until students answer all questions or playing time ends.

Caution and Tips

- You may want to let teams practice rolling first or let them use that first round to really get a feel for it. It's harder than it looks and requires a pretty gentle roll.
- Set clear expectations for how to handle the ball. For example, it is to be *rolled*, not chucked, pitched, kicked, etc.

- As with Hungry Hippos, be prepared for some giggling with the word *ball*. You can consider the "learning spheres" euphemism, but remember to loosen up and enjoy the fun too.
- Set expectations up front about how to respond if someone rolls very badly. Some kids are very uncomfortable with anything that loosely resembles an athletic exercise or requires aiming.
- Keep teams small. Three to four students work best. Any more than that and someone will sit back and ride on his or her teammates' coattails or get off-task.

Variations

- This strategy can be used to go over answers to assignments students completed as homework.
- Students can also match terms and definitions. You give a definition, and students write the term on the ball or vice versa.
- This can be played individually instead of in teams. Each student would have their own numbered ball to use. This does make each round take longer to account for each round of aiming and the assigning of points.

Differentiation Ideas

- Partner students thoughtfully.

Appropriate for

- Worksheets
- Any questions
- Vocabulary

Have you tried Curling? Share using #WorksheetBusters and #Curling.

Giant Grid

The Gist: Students work backward to match answers to the problems on a giant grid.

Why Do It: Playing Giant Grid gets students up and moving, narrows down how many problems they have to do, increases engagement and motivation, and significantly increases the rigor and grit level of traditional worksheets.

Materials

- Plastic sheeting (4 mil)
- Colored masking tape
- Overhead or dry erase markers
- Individual dry erase boards (optional)
- Worksheet or question set and answer key

Directions to Make

1. Spread out the plastic sheeting.
2. Measure out and tape down a grid, 5 ft. x 6 ft., for a total of thirty spaces. Measure spaces 18 in. x 18 in.

Set Up

1. Move desks to leave enough floor space to lay out the grid. Lay grid flat on the floor with enough room around the edges for students to fully access all boxes.
2. Using an overhead marker (recommended) or a dry-erase marker, write one question from your worksheet in each box of the grid. Write large enough to make the problems easy to read. Number them according to the worksheet to make it easy to check answers.
3. Write the answers on sheets of paper (If you insert the paper into plastic sleeves, students can write on them with

dry-erase markers.), one per paper, or on individual dry-erase boards (recommended). Write large enough to make the answers easy to see and leave space to work problems, if applicable.

4. Have the answer key ready for your use. Alternatively, have a roster ready to keep track of how many answers each student gets correct.

To Play

1. Give each student one answer.
2. Students will work out various problems until they believe they have found the match.
3. When they believe they have a match, they stand on the problem that matches their answer. Require some evidence to support their answer, such as the page number they found it on or the work steps to prevent students from randomly guessing spaces.
4. If the student is correct, have him or her initial the paper or board and lay it on the space. If incorrect, the student keeps trying.
5. Once the student has the correct answer, give him or her another answer and repeat the process.
6. Play continues until all spaces are claimed. The student with the most spaces is the winner.

Caution and Tips

- Although I tend to think of this Worksheet Buster as being less like a game than some of the others, my students obsess over Giant Grid and love to play it.
- Some students have very low tolerance for frustration. Try to have them wrestle with the problems as long as possible. When you believe they are at the brink of despair,

you may give broad hints, such as the row or column the matching problem is on.

- As more students find correct matches, the options narrow, making it easier for struggling students to find matches.
- Require showing steps or evidence to prevent random guessing.
- Be prepared with a couple printed copies of the worksheet in case any students choose not to comply with your expectations. This is rarely needed since the physical movement involved with Giant Grid is less intense than some Worksheet Busters.

Variations

- Instead of playing until the entire board is filled, you can set a goal, such as three matches per student. Some students will finish quickly, indicating to you they are successful with the skill. Have an extension activity ready for them to move on to. The spaces will be gone before all students get three matches, but you will know the remaining students need more practice with the skill.

- You can use your roster to keep track of correct answers instead of having students "claim real estate." Then they can turn their answer page or board back in, allowing the game to run indefinitely.
- Giant Grid can be used in a more traditional order—answers on the grid, questions on the papers—but this will lower the rigor and grit.
- You can give all students one problem and have them work silently without getting up to claim their space. Then, at your signal, they all get up to stand on the answer they believe matches. If more than one student claims a space, they must give their argument why their problem matches that answer, and the other students vote which one they believe is correct. Then use the key to check their answers. Correct students sit on their space; incorrect students try again until everyone is seated. Then switch problems and repeat.
- Giant Grid can be used to match vocabulary terms to definitions, capitals to countries, and for other uses beyond worksheets.
- Use Giant Grid as a quick check for understanding or an exit ticket: Write statements about the content or learning in each space and have students stand on the square that best represents them.
- Use Giant Grid as reading response: Put discussion starters relevant to any text (e.g., How did the character change? What impact did the setting have on the plot?) in each square. After reading, students stand in a square they feel they can contribute to. Then discuss.

- Use Giant Grid to play a version of *Connect 4*: Set up using preferred version. Arrange students into teams and give each team its own color of marker. When the team believes they've found a match, they lay down their question or answer and the colored marker to claim the space. When they have four in a row, check for correct answers, returning incorrect matches to play. The first team with four correct matches in a row wins.

Differentiation Ideas

- The fact that spaces get more limited as students claim matches naturally narrows the answer choices for students who are struggling, but you can be mindful of what answers you give students. Be sure to monitor their frustration levels to offer hints when appropriate.

Appropriate for

- Worksheets
- Reading response topics (see variation above)
- Vocabulary

Have you tried Giant Grid? Share using #WorksheetBusters and #GiantGrid.

Candy Land

The Gist: Use a giant version of the classic game board to complete a worksheet. Students complete the worksheet items that correspond to their space on the board.

Why Do It: Students don't often care much about the work they do on a worksheet. Playing Candy Land gets them up and moving, narrows down how many problems they have to do, increases engagement and motivation, and generally breaks up the monotony of a regular school day.

Materials

- Plastic sheeting (4 mil or thicker)
- Permanent markers, large size, six colors
- Square cardboard box or index cards
- Dry-erase or overhead markers
- Worksheet
- Clipboards (optional)
- Construction paper (optional)

Directions to Make the Game Board

1. Lay out your plastic sheeting.
2. Make a template out of cardboard the shape and size you want for your game spaces. They should be large enough for a student to sit on.
3. Plan out your board. To use with a whole class or standard worksheet, you need thirty spaces.
4. Trace your template with permanent marker in the color pattern you desire for your board.
5. Pick a method for students to roll or draw what space to advance to. To make a giant die cube, glue or tape a piece of construction paper for each color on your game board onto the outside of a cardboard box.

NOTE: See below for special instructions if you want to use your box to store the game board when not in use or make a set of color cards by coloring one color on each index card using the same six colors on the board. Students will draw a card and move to the next corresponding color on the board.

Set Up

1. Flip the board over, so the permanent marker is on the back side. This protects it since dry-erase marker erases permanent marker.
2. Number each space using dry-erase or overhead marker. Alternately, you can write worksheet questions directly on the board. Overhead marker tends to erase better. If you have more spaces than worksheet items, you can make bonus or hazard spaces. (See below for suggestions.)
3. Copy or digitally distribute your worksheet if using numbered spaces instead of writing questions directly on the board. Have the answer key ready for you.
4. Have a class roster ready to keep track of turns. Students will wind up out of order around the board, so it can be hard to remember who is supposed to go next.

To Play

1. Students roll the die or draw a card to select a color and move to the appropriate space. The student is the game piece.
2. To stay at that space, the student must answer the corresponding worksheet question correctly. Incorrect students go back to their previous spaces. Students may sit on their spaces when it's not their turn.
3. Keep track of turns on your roster since students will be out of order on the board.
4. Students should record their answers on the worksheet as they go. Clipboards are helpful for this. See variations below for more ideas.
5. The game is over when the first student reaches the end.

Caution and Tips

- If using the box die, make sure students understand and stick to your expectations for how it will be rolled. Although you may see a box, some students might see a soccer ball.
- If students pile up in one area, they may leave their clipboards on their spaces and sit along the edge. Too many bodies in the same area can lead to interpersonal conflicts.
- I tend to prefer activities that allow all students to actively participate at the same time. Often, waiting students become off-task students. It helps to find ways to hold students accountable to paying attention and remaining on-task even while they wait for their next turn.
- To keep students on-task between turns, you can state that all students have to turn in a completed worksheet. If they pay attention during other students' turns, they'll get more of the answers done during the game—encouraging them to stay focused. As each student answers a question, the other students participate by following along and completing their own worksheets.
- Alternatively, you can prepare an exit quiz of questions from the activity, so students have to pay attention during the game to be prepared to pass the quiz.
- If students cannot behave according to your expectations during the activity, they can be sent back to their desks to complete the entire worksheet on their own.

Variations

- Students can complete only the problems they land on, and when the first student wins, they have to walk around and collaborate to get the rest of the items completed from their classmates.

- The game can be played until all students make it through the game board. Students who finish can move on to another activity.
- You can keep track of right and wrong answers on your roster, so you know who may need extra support at the conclusion of the game.
- You can write actual questions on each game space to play without worksheets.
- Do it backwards! Write answers on each space. Students have to correctly guess which question matches it to move forward.
- Play in small groups or teams to cut down on the number of people on the board. This makes the game easier to manage, but it also means more students are waiting (which can lead to off-task behavior). Rotate which member of the team participates on the board. Or better yet, have other learning tasks for students to work on while waiting on their turns.
- For primary students, you can number each space to practice counting numbers and one-to-one correspondence, do the ABCs, identify a word starting with a written letter, sight words, etc.

Bonus Space Ideas

- Candy
- Tell a joke
- Dance break
- Bonus point
- Consequence spaces (e.g., move back two spaces)

Differentiation Ideas

- Some students may not be comfortable being the center of attention as they answer. Choosing a variation where students play in teams may help alleviate that.

Appropriate for

- Worksheets or question sets with clear right or wrong answers

BONUS: Use Your Box to Store the Game

- Glue colored paper on five sides of the box. The sixth side will be the opening.
- You may want to laminate the colored paper for the opening side to make it more durable.
- Cross the box flaps on the opening side three ways, leaving a flap that moves freely. Glue or tape the paper to the edge of that outermost flap.
- Use adhesive Velcro to close that flap to the one beneath it.

Have you tried Giant Candy Land? Share using #WorksheetBusters and #GiantCandyLand.

Cars

The Gist: Leverage the fun of playing with cars to match answers to problems.

Why Do It: What kid doesn't love playing with toy cars? Even big kids do! Use the sheer fun of play to lower the defensive walls and get students to interact with one another and the content.

Materials

- Thirty toy cars (use the cheap ones, hand-me-downs, etc.)
- A strip of plastic drop cloth (use leftovers from making Giant Grid (see page 90), Candy Land (see page 94), or Giant Bull's-Eye (see page 81)
- Colored masking tape or permanent marker
- An assignment and answer key

Directions to Make

- Use masking tape or permanent marker to mark "parking spaces" along the strip of plastic drop cloth (thirty total).

Set Up

1. Cut apart the answer key and tape one answer to each car.
2. Number the parking spaces. If some spaces are unused due to the number of questions on your chosen worksheet, mark them out.

To Play

1. Give each student a copy of the worksheet.
2. Give each student a car or let him or her select one.
3. Students work problems to try and figure out which problem number their answer matches.
4. At your signal, students "drive" their cars and park them in the spaces they believe match their problems. If two cars try to occupy the same space, students must determine which match is correct.
5. Redistribute cars and repeat.

Variations

- Demolition Derby! As an optional way to distribute cars at the beginning of each round of play, give each student a car or have him or her select one. Then they sit in a large circle on the floor, and at your signal, they shove their cars toward the middle to cause catastrophic accidents. You can even allow them to continue grabbing and shoving cars. Then at your signal, they claim the car closest to them as the one they use.
  - Demolition Derby can be used to send students to stations. Number each car (see below) and number station activities around the room. For example, numbers one, seven, thirteen, and twenty-two might all go to one station. Then students go to the stations associated with their cars. You can even interrupt work at a certain point, redistribute cars to mix students back up, then students continue the work the previous group at their new station started. This can be done by putting different worksheets at each station (or essay questions). This will allow students to interact with the content and one another in different ways.
- Allow students to claim their spaces as soon as they have their problems figured out. This narrows the remaining answer choices for students who are still working. You'll need an extension activity for those students to move on to.
- Number the cars by using a strip of duct tape and writing one number on each. Then write the answers on the parking spaces using dry erase marker. Students each get a car using any method, then work on that problem and park the car at the corresponding space. It is easier to work problem-to-answer, and students will work only

that problem instead of the several they would probably work, using the original method above.

- This Worksheet Buster could be used to match vocabulary words and definitions by putting one on the cars and the other on the spaces.

Caution and Tips

- If using Demolition Derby, watch out for smashed fingers. Set clear parameters for how cars may be shoved. Amazingly, some cars seem to have the ability to fly! Others seem to have heat-seeking capabilities.

Differentiation Ideas

- Use color to limit match possibilities. You can write the number on the parking space in different colors and highlight or mark the answer on the cars with the same color. That way, you can also select problems appropriately for students or tip them off on what color they should be looking for.
- If using the variation where students park their cars as soon as they have their problem figured out, it will naturally narrow answer choices for remaining students, providing natural support for students who may need it.
- Teaching primary students? Write a lowercase letter on each car and a capital letter on each parking space. Students can match the letters.

Appropriate for

- Worksheets with objective right or wrong answers
- Vocabulary
- Letter matching

Have you tried Cars? Share using #WorksheetBusters and #Cars.

Board Games

The Gist: Turn any basic board game into a partner or small group Worksheet Buster.

Why Do It: Playing board games to complete worksheets narrows down how many problems students have to do, increases engagement and motivation, and is downright fun. Board games are familiar, affordable, and adaptable. This Worksheet Buster is appropriate for partners or small groups. To play with a whole class, you can set up various board games, so there are enough player roles for each student.

Materials

- Board games
- A worksheet

Directions to Make

- Number the game spaces or pieces one through thirty. For example, on a checkerboard or traditional game board, number the spaces used in play. In Jenga, number the blocks. If there are more spaces or blocks than typical worksheet problem numbers, repeat some numbers.

Set Up

- Set up board games to accommodate all students you want to participate.

To Play

1. Distribute one copy of the worksheet to each student.
2. Divide students into pairs or small groups (appropriate for each game).

3. Students play each board game and complete worksheet problems as determined by game play. For example, if using checkers, students must correctly answer the problem indicated by the number on the space they wish to move to. If using Jenga, students complete the problem indicated by the numbered block they pull out.
4. Play continues until someone wins the game or the teacher calls time. Students turn in their worksheets to be graded.

Variations

- You can place an answer key facedown at each game station. As students complete problems, their opponent checks their answer. If a student is wrong, they must move back to their previous location in the game.
- Some games, like Jenga, can end very quickly (i.e., either accidentally or intentionally). It may be better to designate a playing time rather than playing to a win in circumstances like that. Students can keep track of their wins for a competitive element.
- You can set up different worksheets at different games and students rotate through a few. Once they finish a fairly short game, like Jenga, they move on to another game station. Students can either turn in all their worksheets,

or they can check their work as they go using the answer key variation.

Caution and Tips

- Keep an eye on how well students are playing the games (i.e., they are giving genuine effort and attention to answering the questions, not playing while ignoring the content), so their time is used well.
- Games can be found in garage sales, thrift stores, or by asking for donations. Many people have basic games their kids have outgrown and would be happy to pass along.
- This Worksheet Buster works best with games that are very familiar to students. If they are not familiar with basic gameplay of the board game itself, adding the worksheet element may be too complicated, and students will lose time learning to play instead of spending time on content.
- Games are an excellent opportunity for students to build interpersonal skills.

Differentiation Ideas

- Partner or group students thoughtfully. Because playing board games is a competitive social activity, interpersonal skills are important. Consider how to group students so that positive, productive play is optimized.
- You can also consider the current level of mastery of your students. Do you want to group students of like ability together, so you can address specific learning gaps and provide targeted support? Or do you want a student with developing mastery partnered with a student of more advanced proficiency to allow for some peer learning?
- Different worksheets can be used at each station. Send students to the game station that matches their learning needs.

Appropriate for

- Worksheets with objective right or wrong answers

Have you tried Board Games? Share using #WorksheetBusters and #BoardGames.

Worksheetopoly

The Gist: Students play a giant game of Monopoly to collect "properties" to win the game.

Why Do It: This game gets everyone up and moving and working problems in a fun, incentivized way. The sheer size of this Worksheet Buster definitely piques students' interests! One of the challenges of Candy Land (see page 94) is that not all students are actively completing problems—some are waiting for their turn. Worksheetopoly solves that problem by being so *huge* that all students can fully participate the whole time.

Materials

- Giant sheet of plastic drop cloth (4 mil or thicker and at least 20 ft. x 20 ft.)
- Duct tape or colored masking tape
- Marker
- Square cardboard box (or buy a giant inflatable die—a reasonable DIY-less alternative)
- Dry-erase markers, one for each student
- Yellow and orange poster board (optional)

Directions to Make

1. Cut the plastic to the desired size, at least 20 ft. x 20 ft.

NOTE: I realize this is huge. Either push desks all the way out of the way or arrange to play in the gym, in a common space, etc. Going much smaller puts students awfully close together.

2. Use tape to mark the spaces along the edges, 2 ft. x 2 ft. You'll have ten spaces along each edge (Not counting the corners twice, that's thirty-six spaces total.).
3. Tape all flaps of the box down and use a marker to make the dots of a die.

Set Up

1. Label the spaces as desired. Either write questions directly on the spaces using dry or wet erase markers or number the spaces to represent the assignment. Label remaining spaces as desired, such as Jail, Go, Candy, Go Back Two Spaces, Community Chest (optional), Chance (optional), etc.
2. If using Community Chest and Chance, use the posters to make giant cards. You could write things like *FREE CANDY*, *Swap Places with Any Player*, *Claim One Space Free*, etc.
3. Each problem will need an answer players can check quickly, so copy and cut apart the answer key, write answers out, etc. Place the answer face down or in an envelope at the matching space.

To Play

1. If playing with a numbered game board, distribute a copy of the worksheet to each student. If questions are written directly on the game board, students number a piece of paper and take that with them around the board. Clipboards are helpful.

2. All students start at a square with a problem. They work that problem and answer on their worksheet or on paper. After allowing time for everyone to work, each student checks the problem of the player to their left. Make sure to reset the answer to not give it away to the next player.
3. If a player is correct, he or she writes their name using dry-erase marker on the game board space to "claim" that space.
4. One player rolls the die, and everyone moves that number of spaces to the left (or you can let the roller choose the direction).
5. Continue answering and checking. (See the variations below for ways to "claim" the spaces.)
6. At the end of your designated playing time, the player with the most spaces is the winner.

Caution and Tips

- This board is *big*. If it were smaller, players would be in another's personal space even more than they are at this size. Space out real-estate spaces and include special spaces to give players even more room.
- To have adequate room for this activity, consider using other spaces in your school. Is the gym available? A large-group instruction room? Lobby space? Taking the learning to new locations is a powerful novelty to leverage too! (My awesome teacher friend Erin Scholes developed a close relationship with her school security officers by playing Worksheet Busters in her building's lobby space. The security officers were intrigued and eventually even joined in the fun with her classes. Now they stop by regularly to see what her class is up to.)
- Play should move pretty quickly with little down time, but if students cannot adhere to your expectations, they can complete the worksheet on their own in a traditional way.

Variations

- The simplest version of this game is to number thirty spaces and make the rest bonus or penalty spaces (e.g., Candy, Move Ahead Three Spaces, etc.). This would not require Chance or Community Chest cards, writing questions on the spaces, etc. Students would rotate with their worksheet. Remember, they would still need access to some kind of answer key to check each problem.
- On the other end of the spectrum, you can make the problem spaces into real estate or use the jail option to make this as Monopoly-like as possible.

NOTE: With the jail option, don't allow students to skip a turn, since that would mean not participating in learning, and kids might *want* to go to jail. Try having them give up one of their claimed spaces instead.

- Claiming spaces: You can play so only one student can "claim" one space at a time. When another student correctly answers that space, they replace (or erase) the previous occupant. That way you can allow as many students to claim a space as possible.
- You can use this activity with vocabulary terms and definitions. Write a term on each space and instruct students to define the term to the player to the right, checking as described above.
- For primary students, you can number each space to practice counting numbers and one-to-one correspondence, do the ABCs, identify a word starting with a written letter, identify sight words, etc.

Appropriate for

- All worksheets
- Vocabulary
- Primary work as described above

Have you tried Worksheetopoly? Share using #WorksheetBusters and #Worksheetopoly.

Part 3

LECTURE BUSTERS

Chapter 7

Lecture Is the Salt of Education

Remember, I developed Worksheet Busters to meet teachers where they feel safest—with worksheets they already trust—so they can more confidently and successfully engage their students in meaningful active learning. After launching Worksheet Busters at conferences and online, I started to consider what other teaching routines are trusted but perhaps improvable, creating lulls that were leaving our students passive rather than active.

That brought me to the lecture.

Several years ago, health advice cautioned us to avoid excess salt. Food products started to advertise their low-sodium status, salt alternatives sprung up on grocery store shelves, and commercials for medications illustrated what too much salt had done to our cardiovascular systems. Doctors put patients on low-sodium diets. The message was, “Salt is bad. Avoid it.”

But is it? For much of human history, salt has been the primary way to preserve foods. It was so valuable that it was even used as currency. We get the modern word *salary* from *salt*. Wars were fought over access to it. Our bodies actually *need* it because our bodies' electrical systems send signals through salt. Sodium is even an important element in our hydration, helping maintain healthy electrolyte balances and regulating blood pressure. When Jesus told his followers to be salt of the earth, was he saying he wanted us to be harmful? Cause damage? Be avoided? No, he was saying we need to help preserve, keep a thirsty world healthy, and make a valuable contribution on this earth.

Lecture is the salt of education because current rhetoric leans heavily anti-lecture. Lecture is bad. Good teachers don't lecture. Lecture is boring. Lecture is passive.

Is this true?

Well, it can be.

But it doesn't have to be.

We've all encountered gifted lecturers. Believers of many religions gather regularly to hear someone deliver a message meant to edify them and further their faith. How many of you regularly listen to podcasts? TED Talks are so powerful they've spawned movements and inspired millions. Modern standardized tests even often have a listening feature. Audiobooks and services that provide them are now a multibillion-dollar industry.

Why? If lecture is so boring, so passive, why do so many adults willingly seek out opportunities to listen? When we have virtual reality, video games, and streaming video services at our fingertips, why do we choose to listen?

When lecture is done well, it's powerful. It moves people. And it's memorable.

"I have a dream . . ."

"Four score and seven years ago . . ."

"I am prepared to die . . ."

Like salt, lecture isn't all bad. Does it need to be used carefully, intentionally, and perhaps even in moderation? Yes.

Can it be powerful? Absolutely.

Let's face it—we aren't always teaching thirsty pilgrims seeking divine wisdom. Students aren't necessarily willingly downloading our podcasts to listen in their spare time (And please, if they are, share your magic!). In fact, if you walk into the average classroom during a lecture, you will probably find a number of students checked out, maybe even asleep, or frantically trying to copy the notes before you move on. Remember, we're trying to engage every student, even those who don't want to be at school and likely aren't interested in our content. We *have* to. Our jobs literally depend on it.

Regardless of how gifted we may be as lecturers, we still have to transfer the cognitive load to our students. We know the material, and they need to know it. (And they need to know it beyond just regurgitating facts we've given them.) We want them to truly understand the content. Make connections. Figure out how that information applies to our modern world. Form opinions. Solve problems. Move the world.

At the Association for Middle Level Education Annual Conference in 2015, presenter Julie Adams described learners' brains like buffet plates. She said we walk through the buffet line, piling on more and more information, and at some point, anything else we try to pile on is just going to slide off the top. I don't know about you, but if I'm taking the time to teach something, I think of it as important enough for my students to learn. Slabs of instructional meat sliding off the top just isn't going to work for me. So what's the solution?

We have to provide breaks for students to digest what we've taught them before piling on any more. How frequently we need to stop isn't set in stone—each learner, each developmental stage, and each class environment is unique, so I won't prescribe a number of minutes. I will remind you that adult attention to passive listening tasks—without intrinsic interest—is often measured as minutes in the single digits. What I will recommend is *how* we break and what we do with those breaks.

Often, one suggestion is to offer brain breaks. I get the concept. Let's give kids a moment to get up, move a bit, and then settle back into the learning. It's developmentally responsive. It's beneficial for kids with high adverse childhood experiences (ACEs). It's a good practice, but I want to challenge us to do better.

Now, let me be clear, I'm not against brain breaks, but I don't think they need to be breaks from the learning or disconnected from lessons. Instead, I think we can break the lecture—*bust* the lecture, if you will—and set up learning tasks that require students to construct their own meaning out of what we've just taught. That's what I've designed Lecture Busters to do. Students won't be able to simply regurgitate facts from their notes—they'll have to think. Make connections. Construct meaning. Generate learning.

Those connections provide opportunities for students to continue retrieving material they've previously learned, keeping those concepts relevant and needed, boosting long-term retention. How often have you heard students say something along the lines of, "But that was last chapter! You mean we still need to know that?" We want students to see the bigger picture, to see how one concept is woven in with another, how one idea contributes to another, how one skill builds upon another. But students famously compartmentalize their learning, assuming that one class is completely unrelated to another, one chapter walled off completely from its predecessor, and one lesson is independent of any other.

It's possible to parrot information back without understanding a word of it. But when students have to construct meaning for themselves, their answers can't be found directly in a textbook or in their notes. They have to think.

And isn't that the point?

So in addition to encouraging memorable connections, Lecture Busters also provide valuable feedback for teachers, and we can use it to guide future instruction. As students respond to these activities, we may find that they've grasped the concept so thoroughly that we can safely move on, or we may find that their lack of independent understanding necessitates taking more time on the concept. The students' responses could even reveal misconceptions or gaps in material you've previously covered. These checks for understanding are instructional gold: They provide the critical feedback we need to direct our lessons exactly where students need to go.

Looking back at those professional rubrics used for teacher evaluation, we'll find checks for understanding mentioned there too. In the RISE 2.0 rubric, qualifying for a level three or four on Competency 2.4 requires teachers to check for understanding by asking questions that "push thinking," reveal common misconceptions, and assess mastery at "almost all key moments . . . necessary to inform instruction going forward." Like student engagement, checking for understanding is now an essential component of effective teaching. Regardless of a teacher's own feelings about these concepts, if he or she is going to continue to teach in systems that use these evaluative practices, engagement and checking for understanding are non-negotiable. The value is clear, as is the necessity.

So what makes Lecture Busters different from other checks for understanding? Like Worksheet Busters, Lecture Busters leverage novelty to pique students' curiosity and encourage authentic participation. Lecture Busters require students to make connections and draw conclusions that cannot be found in their notes, necessitating mental engagement. As with Worksheet Busters, Lecture Busters are free, easy to deploy, and applicable to literally any content. In fact, I keep a basket of basic Lecture Buster materials—and a list of Lecture Busters that require no materials—in a cabinet behind my desk to use whenever I feel the need. Most Lecture Busters also have a printable version that's perfect for exit tickets, providing concrete evidence useful in planning the next day's learning activities.

Lecture Busters are also fast. They can be done in as little as three minutes or, if it suits your instructional needs, expanded into a larger activity.

While Worksheet Busters are often physically active, providing engagement of both mind and body, most Lecture Busters don't require as much movement around the room. They are mentally engaging and fun for students, but because they take place largely at the students' desks, there's less management to anticipate. If you found yourself feeling unsure about some of the Worksheet Busters, Lecture Busters will likely feel safer. They are just as valuable, but they meet a different instructional need.

In short, Lecture Busters are checks for understanding that require students to construct meaning from your content in novel ways. Lecture Busters can be planned as part of your lesson but are also readily deployable on the fly with no preparation.

Before we cover any specific Lecture Buster activities, I'd like to lay out some guidelines for use.

1. Please, for the love of God, don't expect students to write while you talk to them. This also applies to videos and reading aloud. Students cannot listen *and* write at the same time. Multitasking is a myth. What's really happening is rapidly switching attention among multiple tasks, and developing brains simply aren't good at this. It is a disservice, and downright harmful, to expect students to listen attentively and write at the same time. Instead, pause the instruction from time to time to allow students to write.

2. There are lots of beliefs about how and when checks for understanding should take place. You are the master teacher in your classroom. I'll leave that to your professional judgment. Suffice it to say that checks for understanding should take place.
3. Lecture Busters are not the only checks for understanding in existence. They are ideas to add to your collection of teaching strategies. As with Worksheet Busters, they serve as a place to start, an inspiration point for your own magic ideas.

Now, without any further ado, let's explore Lecture Busters.

Chapter 8

LECTURE BUSTERS

Alphabet Soup

The Gist: Alphabet Soup is a quick, easy, no-fuss way to give students a chance to pause and construct meaning from your lecture.

The Objective: Students come up with a term starting with the selected letter of the alphabet that relates to what you just lectured about. This requires them to think critically about what you've just taught, connect it to related content, construct meaning from it, and explain their reasoning.

Materials

- Alphabet cards (either flashcards or printed) or alphabet magnet letters

To Play

There are two ways to play:

1. Draw one letter for the whole class to consider. Give students a couple minutes to turn and talk. They should come up with a term that starts with that letter and relates to what you've just covered in a relevant way. After a few minutes, stop their discussion and let pairs share aloud.

Once a term has been shared, it cannot be repeated, forcing remaining partnerships to think deeper. The advantage of this approach is that, by the whole class using the same letter, you're able to compare and discuss the various interpretations of the same idea.

2. Have each partnership draw their own letter and follow the same routine. The advantage to this approach is that some students benefit from the small act of selecting their own item, and then you get to discuss a wide variety of ideas revealed by the diversity of letters in play. However, you don't quite get the stark comparison that happens when so many people get to interpret the same letter.

With either version, I like to have partners share with each other using what I call a "One Minute Mingle." Partners walk the room and have one minute to share with other partnerships, and at the end of the minute, they share not their OWN idea, but rather a DIFFERENT partnership's answer. This encourages them to really listen to each other.

Exit Ticket Version

Name:____________________ Topic:__________

Alphabet Soup Exit Ticket

Identify a term, starting with this letter, that relates to today's topic:

____

letter

Explain how this term relates to today's content:

____

____

____

____

Extend it! Name 2 other terms starting with that letter that also relate to today's topic:

________________ ________________

Find it online at teachbeyondthedesk.com/alphabet-soup.

Have you tried Alphabet Soup? Share using #LectureBusters and #AlphabetSoup.

Junk Drawer

The Gist: Junk Drawer is a quirky way to get students thinking about the content in deeper, broader ways.

The Objective: Students come up with a way to connect a random, unexpected item to your content, stretching them to think deeper about your content, related content, and the broader context.

Materials

- Random items from around your home and garage

OR

- Junk Drawer picture cards (teachbeyondthedesk.com/junk-drawer) cut and laminated. One set makes thirty different cards.

To Play

There are two ways to play:

1. Draw one item (either from your literal "Junk Drawer" collection or a picture card) for the whole class to consider. Give students a couple minutes to turn and talk. They should think of a relevant way to connect it to what you've just covered. After a few minutes, stop their discussions and let pairs share aloud. The advantage of this approach is that, by the whole class using the same item, you are able to compare and discuss together the various interpretations of the same idea.
2. Have each partnership draw their own item (again, either literal or picture cards) and follow the same routine. The advantage to this approach is that some students benefit from the small act of selecting their own item, and you get to discuss a wide variety of ideas and concepts. However, you don't quite get the stark comparison that happens when so many people get to interpret the same item.

With either version, I like to use the One Minute Mingle described on page (see page 124).

Exit Ticket Version

Name:________________________ Topic:____________

Junk Drawer Exit Ticket

Explain how this item relates to today's content:

Item

____

____

____

____

____

Find it online at teachbeyondthedesk.com/junk-drawer.

Have you tried Junk Drawer? Share using #LectureBusters and #JunkDrawer.

Movie Night

The Gist: Movie Night leverages students' love of movies as they pause and explain their learning.

The Objective: Students come up with a movie whose title relates to what you just lectured about or covered in class and explain their reasoning.

Materials

- None! Though you can give students access to lists of movie titles.

To Play

- Allow students to turn and talk to come up with titles aloud, explaining how that title relates to the content. The One Minute Mingle is a great way for students to share with one another before sharing aloud. Set a timer for one minute as students walk around and have brief conversations together. At the end of that minute, I like to have them share an answer they heard from another student rather than sharing their own to encourage active listening as they mingle.

Exit Ticket Version

Name________________________________Topic________________

MOVIE NIGHT

Name a movie title that relates to today's topic and explain.

Movie Title: ______________________________________

How does this topic?

____

____

____

____

Find it online at teachbeyondthedesk.com/movie-night.

Have you tried Movie Night? Share using #LectureBusters and #MovieNight.

#It

The Gist: #It lets students describe their learning using a hashtag.

The Objective: Students come up with a hashtag to describe either their learning or the topic itself.

Materials

- None!

To Play

There are three ways to play:

1. Students can come up with a hashtag to describe the content. This is a great way to summarize and reveal the main idea. Students can share aloud, write their hashtags on whiteboards, or complete the paper exit ticket version

below. A One Minute Mingle is a great way to share with one another before sharing aloud.

2. Students can come up with a hashtag that would have been shared on social media by a person from the lesson's content. For example, they might create a hashtag a historical figure would have posted during the event, a scientist would have posted during a scientific discovery, a character would have shared at that point of the plot, etc. Share as described above.
3. Students can create a hashtag to describe their own mastery of the topic. Having students assess and report on their own learning is a valuable reflective practice, but bear in mind that self-reporting isn't always accurate or reliable. Share as described above.

Exit Ticket Version

Name:______________________________ Topic:________________

#It

Create or identify a hashtag to represent today's lesson.
Circle which you are representing:

The Topic Your Mastery

Hashtag:____

Explain:____

____

____

Find it online at teachbeyondthedesk.com/hashtag-it.

Have you tried #It? Share using #LectureBusters and #It.

Meme Me

The Gist: Meme Me is a fun, entertaining, but insightful way to check in to see what students are learning from your lesson.

The Objective: Students pick or create a meme they feel represents the topic and then explain the relationship.

Materials

- Meme Me pages (optional)

OR

- Several memes (digital or printed)

To Play

There are two ways to play:

1. Allow students to pick a meme (from a digital or printed supply) and explain aloud how it relates to their mastery of the topic.

   NOTE: Be cautious of allowing open searching for memes. Many are far from school appropriate, and it can be hard to keep up with the understood meaning of current pop culture references. One safe option is to print a wide but carefully selected collection of memes and allow students to select from those. Students then share in a One Minute Mingle.

2. Have students create a meme that a person relevant to the lesson would have posted to social media. These could be memes a historical figure would have posted during the event, a scientist would have posted during a scientific discovery, a character would have shared at that point of the plot, etc. The Meme Me printable is helpful for this variation, or students can create a meme on paper or digitally. Again, use digital meme-creation tools with caution

as many include some content not regarded as school-appropriate. Share as described above.

Exit Ticket Version

Name:______________________ Topic:______________________

Meme Me

Draw a meme that represents today's topic.

Explain how this meme relates to the topic.

Find it online at teachbeyondthedesk.com/meme-me.

Have you tried Meme Me? Share using #LectureBusters and #MemeMe.

Hungry Hippos

The Gist: Rather than answering questions you ask, students generate questions about what you've covered. Students have to think deeply about the content to think of a relevant question to ask.

The Objective: Students write a question about what you've covered on a "learning sphere" (see the Hungry Hippos Worksheet Buster, page 53) to provide feedback on their understanding and spur valuable class discussion.

Materials

- Ball pit balls
- Dry-erase markers

To Play

Hungry Hippos may be completed individually, or students may work together in pairs.

1. Students think of a question about what you've just covered. Then they write their question on the ball using the dry-erase marker. This can be a question they believe they know the answer to or something they feel they don't fully understand.
2. Students return the balls to the center of the room. When all balls are returned, they draw out a different ball and return to their seats.
3. Students then consider the question they drew out and think of the answer. Steps 1 through 2 can be repeated multiple times if desired.
4. Call on a few students to share their questions and discuss the answers as a class.

Have you tried Hungry Hippos? Share using #LectureBusters and #HungryHippos.

Six Degrees of Separation

The Gist: Six Degrees of Separation requires students to form connections between two ideas.

The Objective: In the party game Six Degrees of Separation, players try to connect two seemingly unconnected people. In this Lecture Buster version, however, students make connections between content.

Materials

- None, though they may find it helpful to record their chain of connections on the Six Degrees printable (available online at teachbeyondthedesk.com/six-degrees).

To Play

There are two ways to play:

Pause your lecture and identify two pieces of information:

- Two vocabulary terms
- A term and a person
- An event and a person
- A skill and a term
- Two characters
- A character and a term
- A character and an event
- Other ideas, as needed or volunteered

Pick two ideas from your current lecture or pull related material from a previous lecture within related content, so students have to make connections between your current lecture and its broader context.

1. Give students several minutes to talk with a partner about how to connect the two ideas. If needed, copy and laminate a dry-erasable class set of the Homework Buster version below to help students keep track of their thinking. They do not have to identify six steps to the connection; just explain how the two ideas can be connected. Then have partners share their paths to connection.
2. Identify two topics as described above and cold-call a student to start the chain. Then call on additional students or allow them to select the next student to make subsequent

connections. Students will need time to think out the connections before and during this version of the activity.

Exit Ticket Version

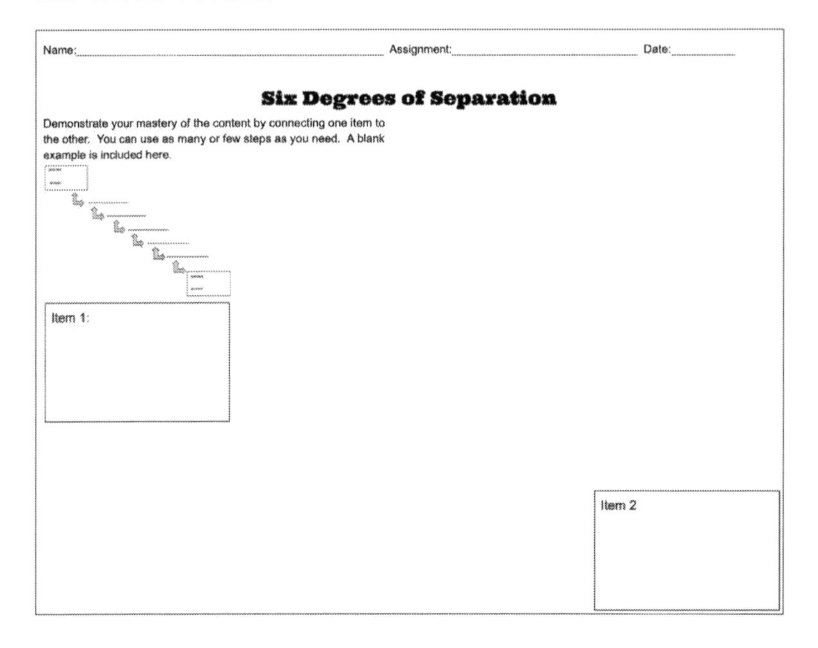
Name:__________ Assignment:__________ Date:__________

Six Degrees of Separation

Demonstrate your mastery of the content by connecting one item to the other. You can use as many or few steps as you need. A blank example is included here.

Item 1:

Item 2

Find it online at teachbeyondthedesk.com/six-degrees.

Have you tried Six Degrees? Share using #LectureBusters and #SixDegrees.

Recipe Card

The Gist: Recipe Card encourages students to consider your current content within its larger context.

The Objective: Students consider the "ingredients" and steps of the topic to create a recipe for it.

Materials

- Printed recipe cards (available at teachbeyondthedesk.com/recipe-card)
- To see Recipe Card used as a Homework Buster, check out (see page 167).

To Play

- Pause your lecture and have pairs of students complete a Recipe Card over what you've just covered. You could even laminate a class set to have readily available and to reuse again and again. Ask pairs to share what they came up with using One Minute Mingle.

Exit Ticket Version

Find it online at teachbeyondthedesk.com/recipe-card.

Name:____________________ Topic/Assignment:__________

Recipe Card

Ingredients:____________________

Steps:____________________

Serve With:____________________

To see some examples of completed Recipe Cards, see page 167. These are from Homework Buster uses of the Recipe Card, so they are perhaps more robust than you should expect from a Lecture Buster response. However, these would serve as good examples to help students understand how to do the Recipe Card.

Have you tried Recipe Card? Share using #LectureBusters and #RecipeCard.

D-Ball

The Gist: Students catch and toss a ball to organize discussion.

The Objective: Discussion is a good way to pause a lecture and draw meaning from the content while providing feedback for the teacher. But discussions can get messy. Some kids talk too much, and some not at all. Some kids sleep, and some blurt every thought that runs through their heads. D-Ball gives kids a tangible reminder to wait their turn and injects a little fun into class discussions.

Materials

- A soft, not-likely-to-hurt-anyone-or-destroy-anything ball

To Play

- Introduce the expectation that no one but the teacher and the student with the ball may talk at any time. Demonstrate tossing and catching expectations (Underhand tosses with clear eye contact are recommended.). This isn't dodgeball, so tosses are meant to be catchable. I emphasize that, since I am not the PE teacher and my class is not PE class, we are not critiquing anyone's tossing or catching skills—no matter how spectacularly they fail. Pose a question and toss the ball to a student. That student answers and then tosses the ball on. The next student may add to the previous response, pose an additional question, or answer a new question from the teacher. Repeat.

Variations

- Balls with questions already on them are available to purchase. If you don't like thinking up questions on the fly or want students to be able to play on their own, this is a good option.
- You can sit in a circle and roll the ball instead of tossing.
- The same procedures can be used to go over study guide questions, assignments, etc.

Have you tried D-Ball? Share using #LectureBusters and #DBall.

Scavenger Hunt Notes

The Gist: Note-taking is typically a passive process. Make note-taking active with this simple adaptation.

Objective: Students search for answers to blanks on the notes around the room.

Materials

- Notes with blanks (e.g., fill-in-the-blank notes, vocab with blank definitions, etc.)
- Answers

To Play

- Before class, tape answers around the room (e.g., on walls, under chairs, etc.). After your lecture or direct instruction, hand out the notes. Release students to search around the room for matches to the blanks on their notes. You'll see "lightbulb" moments as they recognize things from the priming lesson. Then go over the correct answers.

Variations

- Use with notes, vocabulary, facts and dates, sample problems and answers, and more.
- Can be used to go over answers to a worksheet—students look around the room for the answers as they solve problems—or to check their answers.

Have you tried Scavenger Hunt Notes? Share using #LectureBusters and #ScavengerHuntNotes.

Part 4

GRADING

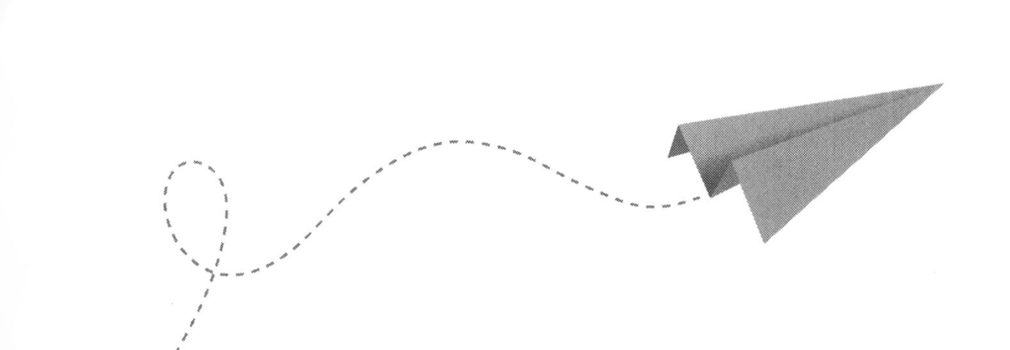

Chapter 9

The Recycling Bin Makes Me Want to Cry

When I served as an instructional coach, a colleague asked me to come observe her class to help her find time to fit an exit ticket into her lesson closure. I timed out the lesson, carefully documenting how many minutes were allotted to each task. As I watched, I found myself growing more and more suspicious of a fairly common lesson routine: grading homework.

Grading homework is the bane of a teacher's existence. Don't we all haul that teacher bag home, full of grading to do, yet let it sit and gather dust as we pass out on the floor while the kids play with LEGO blocks around us (or on us) after supper? Technology helps. There are many sites and services that will quickly grade objective assignments, so we can spend our time in the data. But is a score the same thing as feedback? And what about open-ended work?

Effective feedback has tremendous value. We're finding that students progress more from specific feedback than from any kind of grade. But golly, that takes time.

Time is the elusive unicorn of education, a mythical creature still uncaught.

When we do crack open that teacher bag at the end of a long day and write thoughtful, specific feedback for each of our students, we pass back that work the next day, and where does it go?

Right into the recycle bin.

Sigh.

Long after that teacher and I found the five minutes she needed for an exit ticket, I was left ruminating over grading.

I know many of us use trade-to-grade to quickly score homework, avoiding hauling the work home with us, getting results to students immediately. But after serving struggling students so long, I'm uncomfortable with the lack of privacy in this routine. Sure, we tell ourselves those students don't care that a classmate knows they scored 20 percent on that assignment, but is that right? I don't think so.

I'm also uncomfortable with so much of our already limited instructional time going to a routine that isn't instructive. We might tell ourselves that it is instructive—that as we go over problems with the class, we're correcting misconceptions and reinforcing yesterday's lesson. But are we really?

As I observed in my colleague's class that day, I also watched the students. A few genuinely cared the whole time, and a few more were in and out (They are the ones who will ask to have half a dozen problems repeated. You know the ones.). But many, those who most desperately needed the instructional support, were totally disengaged. Trading to grade in class was passive for those students.

And that's a problem.

So I had a lot to think about. That's when homework became the next instructional routine to be busted.

Some teachers are vehemently against homework. That's fine. Let's agree to respect one another's professional right to assign meaningful homework—or not—and not take up arms against one another over such a thing. Even if you don't assign homework, per se, this section is still for you. At some point, you undoubtedly assign work for your students. They may complete it in class rather than at home. But there are problems they solve, and questions they answer. And you would then go over those answers in class or take them home to go over on your own.

Homework Busters are for you.

When I set out to bust homework, I had a few goals:

- Ease the burden of grading for teachers.
- Provide useful feedback for students.
- Transform a passive classroom routine into a meaningful learning experience.

Homework Busters are activities and procedures designed to turn in-class grading into valuable learning experiences.

Let's end the grade-to-trash cycle and free our profession from the burden of the teacher bag. Let's make grading a powerful, transformative, and instructional practice.

Let's bust the grading routine together!

Chapter 10

HOMEWORK BUSTERS

Post the Answers

The Gist: Students check their assignment against an answer key.

Objective: This activity is specifically designed to facilitate quick in-class grading while maintaining students' privacy.

The Activity: Post an answer key online or somewhere in the room. Students use it to compare their work to the correct answers. Rather than calling out the answers to the whole class, this allows students to check their work quickly and quietly, then you can go over commonly missed problems.

Tips

- Post multiple copies around the room to avoid a chaotic jumble of students.
- This process alone does not drive the learning very deep but does make in-class grading more efficient, so it takes less class time.

- Follow up with an Error Analysis (see page 148) to drive the learning deeper.

Have you tried Post the Answers? Share using #HomeworkBusters and #PosttheAnswers.

Partner Check

The Gist: Students compare their answers with a partner to determine which problems are right or wrong.

Objective: This approach encourages students to investigate whether their answers are correct or not, to defend their reasoning, and to be accountable to actually do the assigned work, so they don't let down their partner.

The Activity: For Partner Check, pair students off and have them compare their answers to each other. When their answers don't match, they reconsider them to try and agree upon an answer. If they cannot agree, they need to be able to justify why they believe their answer is correct.

Tips

- To respect the privacy of students, you may consider allowing them to pick their own partners. (However, we all know how well buddies tend to work together . . .)
- Keeping the same partner for an extended length of time allows for completion accountability—the partner will expect the assignment to be done, so they can participate together.
- For additional accountability, you can have students complete a form like this:

Names______________________________Assignment____________________

Assignment Partner Check

Problems we disagreed on	Answers we had	Correct answer	Why? -Why were we wrong? Or -Why is this answer right?

Find it online at teachbeyondthedesk.com/partner-check.

Have you tried Partner Check? Share using #HomeworkBusters and #PartnerCheck.

Error Analysis

The Gist: After finding out which problems they got right or wrong, students analyze the results to determine the underlying errors.

Objective: The Error Analysis process holds students accountable to really do the work—made up or copied answers won't be enough to complete the form. When a student corrects a missed problem, they have to justify *why* that answer is correct. This process may help them identify repeated mistakes, gaps in their understanding, or something they've misunderstood.

The Activity: After checking their assignment using Post the Answers or Partner Check (see page 145), students complete an Error Analysis form to analyze their own work.

Name:______________________________Assignment:________________

Homework Error Analysis

Problem #	✔ or X	Explain your error.	Justify/prove the correct answer.	What will you do differently next time?

Find it online at teachbeyondthedesk.com/error-analysis.

Tips

- Consider following Error Analysis with Academic Autopsy or Homework Graphic Organizers (see page 156).

Have you tried Error Analysis? Share using #HomeworkBusters and #ErrorAnalysis.

Academic Autopsy

The Gist: When an assignment goes terribly wrong, students complete an Academic Autopsy to determine the cause of death.

Objective: Have you ever taught a concept and then realized it was dead on arrival? Ever graded an assignment and realized, "Yep, I'll be reteaching that one tomorrow!" When our students brutally murder an assignment, they can perform an Academic Autopsy to determine the cause of death and then create a treatment plan, so that never happens again!

The Activity: After grading the assignment using the process of your choice, students who did not master the skill complete an Academic Autopsy form to analyze their errors and hopefully prevent future loss of academic life.

Tips

- A surgical mask and gloves complete the look. Seriously, when's the last time your students got excited after realizing they'd failed something miserably? Dressing the part is an easy, fun way to set the tone and honor your students in their struggle.

Name:____Date:________________

Academic Autopsy Form

You are the Academic Medical Examiner, and you've just received a dead academic skill. Perform an academic autopsy to determine the cause of death.

Identity of the victim (skill or topic)

____

How many wounds (wrong answers) do you see? __________

Analyze those wounds. List the symptoms or anything you notice about these problems.

In the list above, circle the symptoms that those problems have in common. Explain the disease, the error in your original thinking.

____

____

What could you have done differently to treat this disease and save this victim's life?

____

____

Cause of Death (What killed these problems?):

____

Pick one of your missed problems and solve it correctly below, providing evidence to justify your answer.

Find it online at teachbeyondthedesk.com/academic-autopsy.

Have you tried Academic Autopsy? Share using #HomeworkBusters and #AcademicAutopsy.

Homework Quizzes

The Gist: Select a few key problems from the previous night's assignment and use them as a quiz or bell-ringer at the start of class.

Objective: If students feel they need to do the homework to pass the quiz, they'll do the homework. If a student can pass the quiz without doing the homework, did they really need to do the assignment? You're still getting useful data about what your students know and don't know while holding students accountable for their learning without taking class time (or home time) to grade full daily assignments.

The Activity: The day a homework assignment is due, instead of collecting or grading the assignment, give a brief quiz of questions over the assignment. I tend to select five questions from the assignment or three from the assignment with two of the same skill but unique content. Five questions are far easier to grade than an entire assignment. Rather than fussing over getting assignments turned in, tracking down late work, etc., every student who is present participates. This frees you from the typical homework headaches. The quiz itself and its score holds students accountable for doing the work.

Tips

- Use digital tools to get instant results. You can use those results to quickly drive your instruction.

Have you tried Homework Quizzes? Share using #HomeworkBusters and #HomeworkQuizzes.

Homework Gallery Walk

The Gist: You may have done a gallery walk to share projects before. But what about using a gallery walk to grade homework?

Objective: In addition to finding out if their answers are right or wrong, students will analyze assignment content and respond to metacognitive prompts.

The Activity: For a Homework Gallery Walk, place numbered paper, one for each assignment item, around the room. All students take their assignment and start at an item. They write the answer they had for that problem and then rotate to the next item and repeat. Students should initial their contribution each rotation, so you can later look through their thought process.

If their answer is different than what's already been written, they consider whether they are right or made a mistake. If they feel they are right, they contribute their answer. If they feel they are wrong, they write an explanation on the Gallery Walk paper on the wall, describing what they originally did wrong, then correct that problem on their paper.

Rotations continue, and once correct answers are established, students dig deeper into their thinking. Here are some suggested metacognitive questions.

- What is your answer?
- How do you know your answer is correct?
- How do you know your answer is incorrect?
- Show your work, page number, or proof.
- What was your error?
- What is a strategy you used?
- What is a resource you used?
- What could you type into Google to find help for this problem?

- What do you wish you had asked or understood yesterday to be able to do this problem?
- What is an example that would have helped you with this problem?
- What vocabulary terms or skills are important to this problem?
- What did you find easy about the problem?
- What did you find difficult about the problem?
- How did your thinking about the problem change?
- What other homework item is this problem similar to? How are they similar?
- If you gave this problem a title, what would it be?
- How does this problem relate to something else you've learned?
- What questions about this content do you still have?
- What skills might someone need to already know to be able to do this problem?
- What common error did you see with this problem?
- What tip would you give someone who was just learning this content?
- How could you change this problem to make it easier, harder, or deeper?
- Why might you need this skill or knowledge outside of school?

Homework Gallery Walk holds students accountable to do the assignment, so they have something worthwhile to contribute, but even if they didn't do the assignment, participating in this process will expose them to the thinking of their classmates and guide them to think on their own, so they have something to write. Students will think deeply about the content and build connections between concepts, so they understand far more than just a correct answer.

And you know how deeply your students are really understanding your content far more than a letter grade or percentage would say.

Tips

- It's not uncommon for students to struggle with what to contribute next after the correct answer is posted. My favorite solution is to post a page like this instead of blank paper for each problem. I write the problem number at the top, and each box contains a different step or prompt to respond to. As students rotate, they answer the next prompt on the paper, answering the next question for whatever problem they encounter on each rotation.

1) What is the correct answer? Show your work.	2) What do you think the most common mistake on this problem was?
3) What tool, resource, strategy, tip, trick, etc., did you find helpful on this problem?	4) How would you explain how to do this problem to someone else?
5) What do you need to remember to be more successful on this kind of problem?	

Find it online at teachbeyondthedesk.com/homework-gallery-walk.

Variations

- Homework Gallery Walk can even be done in complete silence to force students to explain themselves and argue their thinking only in writing.
- For shorter assignments, supporting struggling students, or real-time collaboration, students can rotate through in small groups.
- This process can also be used to answer questions in class, respond to prompts, go over a test, argue and debate, etc. Try pairing it with Musical Desks (see page 35)!

Have you tried Homework Gallery Walk? Share using #HomeworkBusters and #HomeworkGalleryWalk.

Homework Graphic Organizers

The Gist: For this approach, students create a graphic representation of the relationships between ideas or the steps necessary to solve the problems.

Objective: Understanding how content (both within your own class and in other classes) is all connected is an essential key to students really understanding what we've taught and remembering it far beyond the next test.

The Activity: After marking problems right or wrong, students organize the problems from the assignment to analyze how the various items are related, what content or processes they have in common, what background knowledge or vocabulary they might need, what resources help, etc. Using familiar graphic organizers (e.g., Venn Diagrams, flow charts, etc.), students write problem numbers on the organizers, grouping and arranging them as they see fit to illustrate the connections between problem numbers.

You can assign a certain graphic organizer or allow students to pick their own, based on how they understand the content or process.

Tips

- This is perhaps the deepest of the Homework Buster ideas, and it takes time to build this kind of thinking. Consider starting by creating a class graphic organizer together, then assigning partially completed organizers until students are finally familiar with thinking deeply and can complete one on their own.
- Take it a step further by having students color-code areas of the graph to indicate where they got problems right or where they struggled. Use red for wrong, green for right, and yellow for problems they got right but felt they struggled with. This helps reveal more about WHY a student missed a problem and helps inform us what gaps or misunderstandings need to be addressed.
- Remember, it takes time to develop this kind of thinking. The metacognitive thought prompts from Musical Desks (see page 35) may be helpful.

Name____Date_____________

Homework Venn Diagram

Analyze the content of the assignment by completing the Venn Diagram.
List problems from the assignment in the appropriate areas of the diagram to show which are similar and which are different. Then answer the questions.

Title each section.

________________________ ________________________

Circle how you grouped the problems.

What you needed to know to do them? What process you needed to use to solve them?

Other: _________________________________

Write a statement explaining how those similarities or differences affected how you completed the assignment.

____

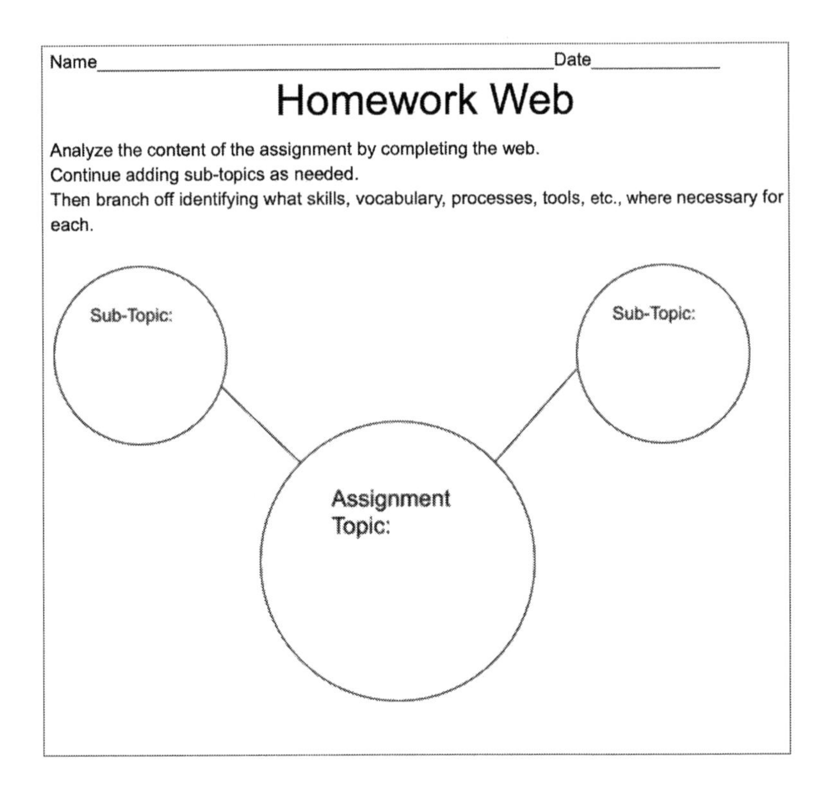
Name____Date______________

Homework Web

Analyze the content of the assignment by completing the web.
Continue adding sub-topics as needed.
Then branch off identifying what skills, vocabulary, processes, tools, etc., where necessary for each.

Name______________________________Date__________

Homework Flowchart

Analyze the content of the assignment by completing the flowchart. Add boxes and arrows as needed.

Topic of the assignment:

What skills or content were involved in that topic?

What did you need to know or do to solve those problems?

Continue the diagram using additional criteria.

Identify where you made your mistakes. Color those areas RED.

Where you were confident and successful, color those areas GREEN.

Where you were unsure or lacked confidence, color those areas YELLOW.

Find them online at

teachbeyondthedesk.com/homework-graphic-organizers.

Have you tried Homework Graphic Organizers?
Share using #HomeworkBusters
and #HomeworkGraphicOrganizers.

Homework Sort

The Gist: Students think about what's being asked on the assignment to organize problem numbers into categories or groups.

Objective: This activity requires students to make connections between individual problems within an assignment. We know these connections are important to really understanding the content, remembering it longer, and being able to transfer knowledge to new contexts.

The Activity: Make one set of problem cards (simply, the numbers one through thirty, printed and cut apart) for each student.

> **NOTE:** These will be reusable, so card stock may make them more durable.

Pair this with Post the Answers or Partner Check. Students check their answers on their assignment and then use a Post-It note flag to mark the number cards for problems they got wrong (red) or struggled with (yellow).

Then students consider the content of the assignment items and sort the number cards into groups.

Examples

- People, places, and events
- One-step equations vs. two-step equations
- Problems with one solution, no solution, and infinite solutions
- Characters, setting, plot, and theme

You may have categories in mind or leave it totally open-ended to see how students are thinking about the content.

Tips

- As an alternative to making number cards to represent the problems, students can use dry-erase materials to write the problem numbers or use a form like this.

Name:____________________ Assignment:____________ Date:______

Homework Sort

Sort the assignment problems into categories. Consider how different problems are related. What skills, knowledge, steps, or resources did you need to complete each problem? How do some problems connect to other problems?

Draw your groups here. Mark problems you missed with an **X** and ones you found difficult with an **!**. Label each category.

Example:

Look at where your flagged problems fell in your categories. Draw a conclusion about the problems you missed.

____

____

____

Find it online at teachbeyondthedesk.com/sorting-homework.

- The thought prompts used with the Gallery Walk Homework Buster might be helpful in encouraging students to consider these connections.
  - What strategy did you use?
  - What resource(s) did you use?
  - What vocabulary terms or skills are important to this problem?
  - What other homework item is this problem similar to? How are they similar?
  - If you gave this problem a title, what would it be?
  - How does this problem relate to something else you've learned?
  - What skills might someone need to already know to be able to do this problem?
  - What was a common error with this problem?
  - Why might you need this skill or knowledge outside of school?
- Students may find it helpful to use resources (e.g., their textbook, notes, designated websites, etc.) to find out more about the content to be able to make connections.
- If a student feels a homework question belongs in more than one category, it is up to you whether you make them choose (or reconsider their categories) or include it in multiple places. There are benefits both ways.
- This activity is similar to the Graphic Organizer and Six Degrees of Separation Homework Busters. Those Homework Busters also require students to make connections between homework problems.
- When students have finished grouping their problems, they can take a picture of their groups, record their explanation, and post that to an online learning platform. You

could walk around the room and talk to them about their categories, marking students who need additional practice on a roster. Regardless, students will discover what they got right and wrong, and you'll find out who's got it and who doesn't. Additionally, students will go deeper with the content than a traditional assignment would.

Have you tried Homework Sort? Share using #HomeworkBusters and #HomeworkSort.

Six Degrees of Separation

The Gist: Six Degrees of Separation, Homework Edition is similar to the Lecture Buster version (see page 132). You may have heard of Six Degrees of Kevin Bacon, a theory that any two people on earth are connected to Kevin Bacon in six connections or less. The homework edition of this game similarly theorizes that any two questions are related in six connections or less.

Objective: Students explore how to connect two problems from an assignment. This will require them to break down the skills needed to solve the problem, steps they used to complete it, and how the problem fits into the overall topic of the assignment.

The Activity: There are several ways to use this strategy. One is a partner activity covering the entire assignment, and the other is individual and grades two teacher-selected problems from the assignment.

For the partner version, assign each student one problem from the assignment. Pair students off. Partners compare their answers to both problems and agree on the correct answers. Then they discuss how those two items are connected. Share the thought prompts from Musical Desks (see page 35) and examples (below) to encourage students to make connections. At the end of your designated time, each partnership shares how they connected their two problems. You can play again by assigning different problems or having students keep their problem but work with a different partner to make brand new connections.

Have fewer problems than students? Duplicate the numbers you're using. Multiple students can do the same problem and be paired with a different number to form an entirely different connection. Or multiple pairs can do the same problems and compare connections.

You can have partnerships fill out the form that goes with the teacher-selected version or play the game to help students get the idea, then have them do the teacher-selected form for you to grade.

The teacher-selected form used allows you to grade two key problems from the assignment. Prior to using, consider the assignment and pick two significant problems. Indicate them on the form or on the board. Students then complete the form and turn it in, allowing you to see their answers to the two problems and also evidence of their understanding of the rest of the assignment and covered content. This could even be used as a bell-ringer at the beginning of class to kill two birds with one stone—metaphorically speaking, of course.

Name:________________ Assignment:________________ Date:________

Six Degrees of Separation

Demonstrate your mastery of the content by connecting one item to the other. You can use as many or few steps as you need. A blank example is included here.

Item 1:

Item 2:

Find it online at teachbeyondthedesk.com/six-degrees.

As you can see from these examples, there's not one right path. The value of this exercise for you, as the teacher, is to see your students' thinking. Some may connect the problems literally. Some may connect the processes. Some may pull knowledge from beyond the assignment. You're not just checking two homework problems; you're glimpsing their thought processes.

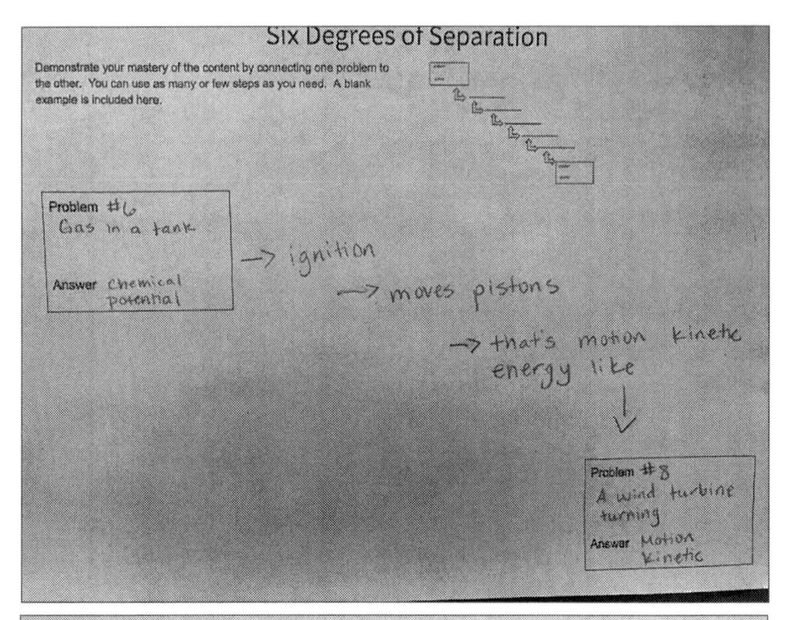

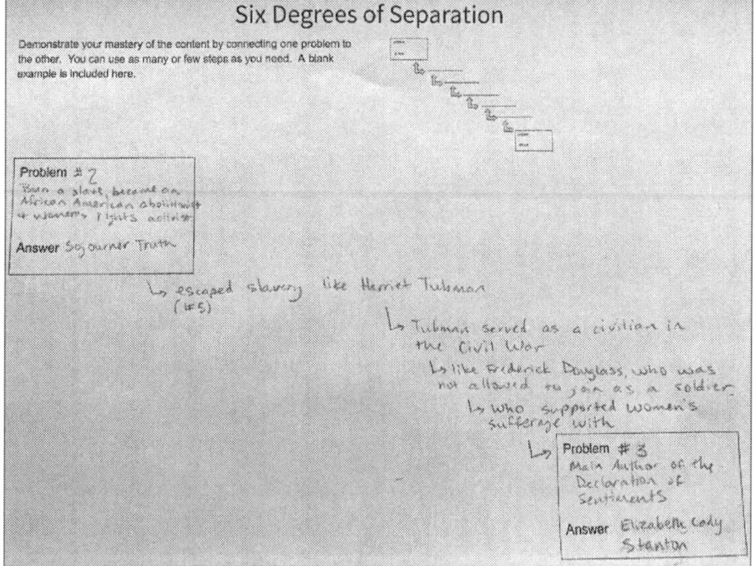

Tips

- Students may find it helpful to use resources (e.g., textbook, notes, designated websites, etc.) to learn more about the content to be able to make connections.

- You could also use Six Degrees as a Lecture Buster without a worksheet. See page 131 for more.

Have you tried Six Degrees? Share using #HomeworkBusters and #SixDegrees.

Recipe Card

The Gist: The Recipe Card, used in Lecture Busters (see page 133), can also demonstrate mastery of the process or relationships between problems on an assignment.

Objective: For Recipe Card, students either consider the "ingredients" of an assignment and the steps to complete it *or* the ingredients of the content and the steps leading up to the event, the creation, or the discovery of the content.

The Activity: If the assignment is process related, students list the individual skills necessary to complete the steps of the process as ingredients. Then they describe the steps to complete the process. Finally, they list related skills in the "serve with" portion of the recipe card.

If the assignment is about content rather than process, students can list the "ingredients" of that content (e.g., important terms, events, people, skills, etc.). For the steps, they list the "steps" leading up to that content—what "preheated the oven," led to the content, etc. For the "serve with" section, students list related content, terms, topics, etc.

Name__________________________________ Topic/Assignment:

Recipe Card

Ingredients: ____

Steps: ____

Serve With: ____

Find it online at teachbeyondthedesk.com/recipe-card.

Tips

- When first introducing Recipe Card, share examples, so students understand what to do.
- Don't forget, this activity can also be used as a Lecture Buster! Pause your lecture and have pairs of students create a recipe card to explain what you've just taught. See more on page 133.
- To use Recipe Card as a Homework Buster, have students complete a recipe card in class the following day. Collect and consider the recipe cards to get a better understanding what your students know, how they understand the topic within its larger context, etc. Pair Recipe Card with Post the Answers or Partner Check to quickly assess the assignment before students start their Recipe Card. You can collect both the assignment and the recipe card if

you feel you need to, but the Recipe Card alone will give you ample evidence of understanding.

- Recipe Card can even be used for book reports or to summarize text!

Name ______ Recipe: WS 46: 2-Step Equations

Recipe Card

Ingredients: variables, co-efficients, constants, inverse operations, operations, equal sign

Steps: 1. Locate the variable
2. Add or subtract the constant
3. Repeat on the other side of the equal sign
4. Multiply or divide the co-efficient
5. Repeat on the other side of the equal sign
6. Plug the answer back in to check

Serve With: integer operations

Name ______ Topic/Assignment: The Revolutionary War

Recipe Card

Ingredients: 15 colonies, British rule, Lexington and Concord, Stamp Act, Tea Act, "taxation without representation," tariffs, Boston Massacre, George Washington, Samuel Adams, Patrick Henry, Continental Congress, Declaration of Independence, Bunker Hill

Steps: 1. Preheat with British rule and increase taxation without colonial representation
2. Add violence between soldiers and militia
3. Start forming a group of Continental leaders
4. Declare independence
5. Start a war

Serve With: The Magna Carta, The U.S. Constitution, The Revolutionary War

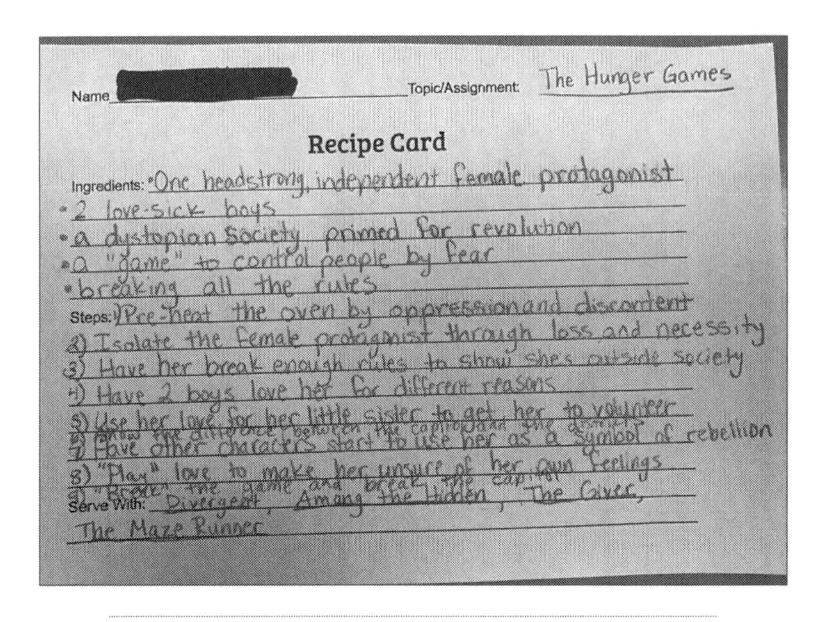

Name ____________ Topic/Assignment: The Hunger Games

Recipe Card

Ingredients:
- One headstrong, independent female protagonist
- 2 love-sick boys
- a dystopian society primed for revolution
- a "game" to control people by fear
- breaking all the rules

Steps:
1) Pre-heat the oven by oppression and discontent
2) Isolate the female protagonist through loss and necessity
3) Have her break enough rules to show she's outside society
4) Have 2 boys love her for different reasons
5) Use her love for her little sister to get her to volunteer
6) Show the difference between the capitol and the districts
7) Have other characters start to use her as a symbol of rebellion
8) "Play" love to make her unsure of her own feelings
9) "Break" the game and break the capitol

Serve With: Divergent, Among the Hidden, The Giver, The Maze Runner

Have you tried Recipe Card? Share using #HomeworkBusters and #RecipeCard.

Bull's-Eye Answers: Homework Edition

The Gist: Use the Giant Bull's-Eye (see page 81) to sort answers to homework questions.

Objective: Students use the rings of a bull's-eye to analyze answers to a question and sort them as far from right all the way down to the best-fit answers.

The Activity: This activity uses the Giant Bull's-Eye from the Worksheet Buster (see page 81).

To use the Bull's-Eye as a Homework Buster, the rings are used as follows:

- The outermost ring is for answers that are FAR from correct. They may be factually incorrect, untrue, or otherwise obviously not correct.

- The next ring is for answers that are true or factually correct, but don't quite answer the question being asked. For math questions, this might be answers that used parts of the correct process but contained errors that led to an incorrect answer.
- Then the next ring is for answers that seem correct, both factually and in the context of the question. I call this the "shopping cart." You know how, when you're shopping, you see a shirt you THINK you like, but you're not sure? What do you do? Well, I carry it around with me through the rest of the store. Put it in my shopping cart! Then I decide if I really want it or not as I see the rest of the merchandise and take time to weigh this option. So this ring is the answer shopping cart. We gather answers we *think* may be right.
- Then we compare those options in our shopping cart and isolate the one(s) that are the BEST, most complete, for the question. For math questions, this would mean not just a fully correct answer but correct, clear steps as well.

To Play

- Pick one significant question from the assignment.
- Each student writes his or her answer on an index card or scrap of paper. You collect them. Then group students into small groups, ideally around three students per group. Shuffle the cards up and then distribute one per person to each group. The groups consider each answer and place them on the bull's-eye according to the descriptions above. The whole class gets a visual, interactive way to consider the content and nail down the "best" answers. By not writing names on the cards, students get to evaluate

other students' answers and realize where their own falls, etc., while respecting their privacy.
- Repeat with any other essential questions.

This gives the students immediate feedback they discover on their own and with their peers about their own answers. You are also getting immediate feedback which problems seem particularly error-ridden, what the common errors are, and what distinguishes an almost-right answer from a completely-right answer. This feedback can drive future instruction and re-teaching.

Tips

- Consider closing with a metacognitive, reflective journal. Have students reflect on where their answers fell on the bull's-eye, why, and what they now realize they could have done to improve their answers.
- This bull's-eye can be used as a Worksheet Buster (see page 81) to help students narrow answer choices to select the BEST answer. It's an excellent strategy, and the big, plastic version gets them up and moving!
- The Curling Homework Buster (see page 86) also uses this giant bull's-eye and is a fun, competitive way to do an assignment in class.

Have you tried Bull's-Eye Answers: Homework Edition? Share using #HomeworkBusters and #BullsEyeAnswers.

Pass It, Math It

The Gist: Students expand answers by adding, subtracting, or dividing their answers.

The Objective: This activity leads students to think deeply about their answers in out-of-the-box ways.

The Activity: Students pass their work one student to the right. Identify a problem for students to evaluate. Then you call out a math operation (see below). Students perform that operation on the identified problem. Repeat, passing again, identify a new problem, and continue with any operation. At the end of designated play time, students get their original work back and review the thoughts of their classmates using Greatest Common Factor, discussing as appropriate.

Operations

- Addition: Add something to their answer to make their answer stronger.
- Subtraction: Take something away from their answer to make their answer stronger.
- Division: Rearrange their answer (or steps) to make their answer (or process) stronger.
- Greatest Common Factor: Analyze all the input students have provided. What do they all have in common?

Tips

- Any deep thinking like this can take practice. Perhaps have the whole class try each operation on the same problem to familiarize the students with them before actually playing.
- What is added, subtracted, or rearranged can be evidence, details, steps, etc.
- This activity is best suited for problems that are open-ended or may have more than one way to solve.
- This activity can be used on open-ended, essay, or multi-step problems. Again, students can work the same problem and consider multiple students' thinking by passing or

can work different problems and consider many different problems by passing.

- "Operations" can be customized to your content or teaching style.
- "Operations" can be pre-planned or randomized. Consider writing them on a die, putting them on a random spinner, or drawing them out of a bag. Random spinners are available online, such as wheeldecide.com.

Have you tried Pass It, Math It? Share using #HomeworkBusters and #PassItMathIt.

Part 5

BUST THE BOREDOM

Chapter 11

I'm Not the Magic

I know what it's like.

I've been the one in the chair through bad professional development (PD). I've been the one sitting there, thinking, "My school paid for *this*?" or "I could be getting *so much done* right now." And I've been in the seat for good PD, excited and energized by the ideas presented, but then left overwhelmed with what's already on my plate, and those exciting new ideas gather dust in my notebook instead of breathing life into my classroom.

This book will have been a waste of your time and money if it feels like bad PD. It's even a waste if you found good ideas but will just let it gather dust on your shelf.

Let's face it; I'm not the magic in your classroom—you are.

I want this book to empower, encourage, and energize you. You are the master teacher, the expert in your classroom. You have your own unique teaching style and your own strengths and weaknesses. Though there are a few universal best practices out there, you should be skeptical at best—and flee from at worst—any book that tells you exactly how *you* should teach. You are you.

Right?

Have you ever read a book or sat in a workshop where you're left thinking you're supposed to teach exactly like Famous Teacher Author Person? I have.

I think one of the best things about our profession is the fact that there are so many ways to do it well. You may teach next door to someone who teaches the same content and the same grade in very different ways, and you both do it well. I think that's amazing. I love that we're in a field that lets us use our creativity, interests, talents, and knowledge to create entirely unique learning experiences for our students. I love that there's no one right way to do it.

Let me be very clear: I do not think you need to teach like me. The way I teach works for me because I'm me. You are not me. I am not you. Though we can agree on a few universal best practices, I will not prescribe a specific way to teach. Let's agree that we need to engage our students in deep, meaningful learning. Let's agree to check for understanding to drive our instruction where our students need to go. And let's agree to try and make grading a valuable learning experience. What I have presented in this book is not to be regarded as a full treatise on what great teaching looks like. Instead, I hope you consider these ideas like the sample cups you get at a frozen yogurt bar. Get a taste, get inspired, and then craft your own creations.

I believe the ideas you'll use the most and best are ideas you create yourself. You will have made them to be the best for your classes, your content, and your teaching style. You will be comfortable with them. You will be proud of them. You will be excited by them. And you should be! I hope the ideas presented so far are scalable and adaptable so that you can tweak them—at least some of them—to suit your instructional needs. But I don't want that to be where we stop. My true goal and ultimate dream is to empower teachers to create their own activities.

I once heard Dave Burgess say in his Teach Like a Pirate presentation that people think inspiration is like lightning that just falls on some people and misses others. His point was that creativity isn't like that, that anyone can be creatively inspired. But I sat there, sheepishly looking from side to side, slightly worried, because it *is* like that for me. Ideas tend to just appear in my brain, often right before I go to bed. Sometimes I encounter something that sparks an idea for me. I think I am naturally creative. And I get that not everyone is. But even my "lighting-strike" ideas aren't ready for a class of thirty twelve-year-old students. If there's any weakness, any chink, they'll find it. They'll exploit it. And they'll eat me alive.

Inspiration is sometimes magical, yes. Turning that inspiration into a functional, successful classroom activity isn't. That's a process anyone can follow.

Every idea presented in this book has been through a fine-tuning process. From initial inspiration to workable classroom activity, I put each idea through a series of steps. Whether you're naturally creative or not, you can follow those steps. I'd like to share my process with you, so you can craft your own Buster activities and be empowered to bring even more magic to your own classrooms.

Chapter 12

The Process

The Inspiration

Beyond the lightning-strike ideas, I have found inspiration in materials I have on hand, classic games, or specific learning needs.

Paper Airplanes, Speed Dating, and Q and A were all inspired by the question, "What can I do with just a worksheet?" Interval Races, Alphabet Soup, Giant Grid, and Curling were all created using materials I already had.

Party games inspired Musical Desks, Heads-Up Seven-Up, Go on Six, and Hungry Hippos.

I created Sorting Activities, D-Ball, and Strike a Pose to address specific learning needs, namely to get students up out of their desks to increase participation or to make learning more tangible and hands-on.

Sometimes I come up with activities because I want to make something I already do better. I try to improve something about my instructional routine that seems lackluster. Giant Bull's-Eye,

Academic Autopsy, and Scavenger Hunt Notes were all born out of this quest.

The Rules

I follow some basic rules. I require that my Buster ideas:

- Should not be expensive, complicated, or time-consuming to prepare.
- Should be readily applicable to any learning content, not tied to one specific concept or skill.
- Should involve all students, because waiting students are not engaged students.
- Should make learning more meaningful, deeper, or more engaging. This is not fluff fun for fun's sake.

There are perfectly good ideas out there that don't meet these rules, but remember: Busters are meant to be applicable to any content, easily adaptable, scalable, and affordable. That's what makes a Buster a Buster. These rules help keep Busters that way.

The Questions

After an idea takes shape, I start to consider how that idea might work in a real classroom. I ask myself a series of questions to help identify potential weaknesses and plan for the kinds of problems that may arise.

- How can I utilize a worksheet and answer key?
- What games do the students already know, and how can I use them?
- What materials can I easily get?
- How do I work around the space of my room?

- What is the purpose of the activity? Is it to provide data, get a graded assignment turned in, observe students as they work, or practice a skill?
- How do I ensure all students are participating all the time? What makes them want to or what holds them accountable? What are the roles?
- What rules do I need? What do I do if someone doesn't follow them? What's Plan B?
- How does this make the learning deeper, more effective, or more memorable than the original worksheet?

The First Test Run

When I'm ready to test it in the classroom . . .

- I usually deploy a new idea with as much safety as possible. I tell my students in advance that we'll be trying something new.
- I keep it short, just a couple of rounds, enough that students start to understand what's going on but not so much that I potentially tank a whole day of learning.
- I try a new idea far enough into a unit that students aren't depending on the activity to truly learn the concept or skill. Test review is perfect.
- I type out and share or project rules and expectations as clearly as I can. I try to anticipate *everything*—keeping in mind that I don't actually know exactly what to anticipate—to keep the activity as clear for the students as possible.
- I take notes as it goes. (If I'm too frantic as I run it to take notes, I know it's not right yet!)
- Finally, I conference with students after. I ask what worked, what didn't, and why.

The Post Mortem

Sometimes those test runs fail. But that doesn't mean I chuck the idea entirely. Why do ideas fail?

- Maybe an activity is just too new. New activities may take a few tries before they really make sense to the students and run smoothly. So we may just need to try them again.
- A test run may reveal a problem I didn't anticipate; from unexpected wait time for students to materials not working right, there are potential pitfalls we just don't always see until we're knee-deep in the activity.
- The activity may not be quite right for the content or the students (or even our teaching style). Perhaps a simple tweak will help. Maybe it is louder than we're comfortable with, our class wound up handling the movement poorly, or the value of the content got lost in the hullabaloo of the activity. We might just need to tweak the activity process to better respect our own learning environment.
- The activity may fail because it just isn't a good idea. Perhaps I'm forcing an activity just because I like a material, or the fun outweighs the learning, or there's just no way to keep all students involved. Sometimes an idea is just a bad idea.

I caution you to not reject any idea too quickly after failure, even if it seems like the idea falls into that last category. One attempt is rarely enough, and most ideas really can be good. So work at them. Tweak them. And try again. Go back to Chapter 3 and give it a quick reread. Maybe an idea does need to be rejected outright. But really, if you were inspired by something, chances are there's good in it!

Failure makes us so uncomfortable. It feels embarrassing. And because we're teachers, we have quite an audience for that failure. A failed activity can be a classroom management nightmare. It's easy to want to throw in the towel and go back to the safety of the way we've always done things. But please don't stop there. Take diligent notes. Reflect. Go back to the drawing board. And then try again.

Some of the Busters in this book failed miserably the first time I tried them. My first attempt at Heads-Up Seven-Up was an organizational nightmare. I didn't realize I would have to make sure the "up" problems had matches in play. I hadn't anticipated the downtime most of the class would experience after students were selected and were guessing who tagged them. It was definitely *not* a fun experience for me! I found myself stressed and frantic. I hated it. In fact, I even tabled the idea for a while. But it had value, so I went back to it. Those problems were solvable. Though I still find those aspects to be the trickier parts of that activity, now that I know they exist, I can do something about them. The activity I initially hated eventually became a favorite for some of my students (and some participants in my workshops).

Most of the time, rather than failing miserably, an activity just needs some tweaks. The trial run of Paper Airplanes revealed that not all students know how to make an airplane. It also revealed that I need to clearly stipulate my expectation that they keep those planes tucked safely in their fingers until launch time. That's why I addressed those issues in the instructions for Paper Airplane.

Sometimes I'm totally blindsided by an issue. I had been using Musical Desks for years before a class showed me that I have to specify how one enters a desk. This particular class dove across desktops, climbed under desks, and turned the classroom into a veritable parkour course. Again, if you look back over those directions, you'll see that I now address this desk-entering skill.

My least favorite kind of failure, though, is when I know the failure is me. Although I'm very comfortable with students moving around the room, I don't like it to get loud, and it turns out I have some pet peeves I never would have known about if students hadn't discovered them for me. Hungry Hippos has taught me that I cannot stand students bouncing balls on the floor. I don't mind students tossing them lightly or rolling them on the desks but bouncing them on the floor drives me crazy. I had no idea until I deployed Hungry Hippos! I didn't notice it the first time or even the second. In fact, it wasn't until my second or third year using Hungry Hippos that I put two and two together and realized the reason I felt so antsy and tense after Hungry Hippos was the doggone bouncing of balls. Well, that was an easy enough problem to solve! By then, I'd been using Hungry Hippos long enough to truly love it, so I wasn't going to reject it just because that irritated me. Instead, I established new rules about how those balls were to be handled, and now I collect them as students work.

I've included a document of these prompts and questions that may help as you design your own activities.

Create Your Own Buster

The Inspiration

- ❏ A material:
- ❏ A game:
- ❏ A specific learning need:

The Rules

- ❏ Should not be expensive, complicated, or time-consuming to prepare.
- ❏ Should be readily applicable to any learning content, not tied to one specific concept or skill.
- ❏ Should involve all students. Waiting students are not engaged students.
- ❏ Should make learning more meaningful, deeper, or more engaging. Not fluff fun for fun's sake.

The Questions

- How can I utilize a worksheet/answer key?
- What games do they already know that I could use?
- What materials can I easily get and use?
- How do I work around the space of my room?
- What is the purpose? Provide data? Get a graded assignment turned in? Observation while students work? Practice?
- How do I get all students participating all the time? What makes them want to or holds them accountable? What roles are there?
- What rules do I need? What do I do if someone doesn't follow them? What's Plan B?
- How does this make the learning deeper, more effective, or more memorable than the original worksheet?

Materials:

Rules:

Objective:

Post-Mortem Notes:

- What was successful?
- What wasn't?
- What stressed me or didn't run smoothly?
- Where did students get confused?
- What were my students' thoughts?
- Was the learning target clear and well-supported by this activity?
- Do I need to try this again before I make changes?
- What unexpected problems did I encounter?
- What tweaks do I need to make?
- Who can I tag in to help me make this more successful?
- Have I gone back to re-read chapter 3?

Find it online at teachbeyondthedesk.com/tips.

As you try out these Buster activities and roll out your own, you're bound to encounter failure. Don't let that be the end of the story. Use Chapter 3 as a resource, along with the process laid out in this chapter, to reflect on what went wrong and refine your ideas, so they're more successful.

You are the magic in your classroom. Your students are counting on you to be that magic every day. Whether you currently teach using out-of-the-box methods or lean heavily on your textbook and blackline masters, you are called to engage your students in meaningful learning.

Be the magic.

They're counting on you.

Chapter 13

"No" Won't Kill You (Probably)

I want to close our time together by sharing my journey from teacher to professional presenter and author.

In February 2015, the Association for Middle Level Education (AMLE) sent out a call for presentations for the 2015 Annual Conference.

I kept that email open on my desktop for two weeks.

At the end of the day, I'd close out my tabs and programs and then find that email window still open. I'd look at it, think about it, and then get butterflies in my stomach. I'd think about closing that email window out, but then I'd hesitate. Finally, I'd sigh, shutting down my screen but still keep that window open to deal with another day.

For two weeks, I fought with that window. I *really* wanted to present. I'd presented at local and regional conferences before, often something about technology, and I knew I really enjoyed presenting. But I was cowed by the fact that I was nobody. I wasn't famous. I was just some teacher from Indiana. What could I bring to the table that wasn't already being said by someone else?

Someone better? Yes, I knew I was a good teacher. And I knew there were a number of things I did well. But a big, national conference like that seemed to belong to the famous, the somebodies. And I wasn't anybody.

But still, I wanted it.

One day, as I ran through that close-out-the-windows-for-the-night routine, I found that email again. And I resolved, "If the worst they can tell me is 'no,' what's the harm in trying?"

If the most I had to fear was rejection, how bad could it be? I mean, if I never tried, I wouldn't present. If I tried and was rejected, I wouldn't present. The outcome would be the same. So why not try? Rather than risking failure, it felt, instead, like risking a chance.

A chance to present.

A chance to do something new.

A chance to do something great.

So I sat back down, rolled my chair up to the desk, and clicked the link to open the presentation form.

At first, I had no idea what to do. I flipped through my mental catalogue of what I thought I did well, but I was very aware of how many experts were already successfully presenting messages on the same things. What could I bring that was new? What message did I have that was uniquely mine? That's when I thought of the activities I'd done for years that leverage readily available materials to make learning more active and fun. At this point, I didn't call them "Busters" of any kind. In fact, the title I submitted under that year was "Prep-Once Activities: Activities You Make Once and Easily Adapt for Many Uses."

Because I had never presented at a national conference of this caliber, I opted for the smallest presentation format, a speed session where I would present the same fifteen-minute spiel three times.

I filled out the form, clicked "submit," and waited. And then, in April 2015, I received the email that my session had been selected.

The AMLE Annual Conference was in Columbus, Ohio, that year. I was a bit of an oddball in the speed session room, spreading my plastic sheeting activities across the floor, but my oddities attracted a lot of attention, and my session was well-attended. We flew through our fifteen minutes together, and I had a blast. I was probably grinning from ear-to-ear the entire time. Seriously, it was incredibly energizing! After my last session, as I was folding up my materials and returning the many chairs we'd "borrowed" from other tables, a guy in red shoes approached me. He introduced himself as Dru Tomlin, then the director of middle level services for AMLE. He asked if I'd considered presenting a concurrent session at AMLE2016. At that time, I was so unsure if I'd been successful with AMLE2015 that I could do little more than stammer for a moment. But I finally choked out an agreement. If AMLE would have me, I'd happily be back for more.

To test-drive the concurrent-length version of my session, I presented at a smaller, regional conference that winter. Again, my session was well-attended, and I got practice timing out the longer session and developed a better understanding of how to explain my activities to a live audience of teachers. One major takeaway was that I wanted the concurrent length to feel as active and energetic as the speed session had. When the call for presentations came out that spring, I submitted a proposal for a concurrent session, using the title "Worksheet Busters" for the first time. A second concurrent session was also accepted, the debut of what are now known as "Homework Busters." Between the 2015 and 2016 Annual Conferences, I wrote an article about some of my activities for the AMLE magazine.

After the AMLE2016 Annual Conference, I presented a webinar for AMLE. At the conclusion of the webinar, I was given the opportunity to join AMLE's team of experts for on-site professional development. And let me tell you, that term *expert* still makes me uncomfortable.

Soon after, I was invited to be a "Trailblazer Presenter" at AMLE2017. The following year, I was a featured presenter in Orlando for AMLE2018. I had already started writing this book at that time, with no publisher or contract, and had shared Worksheet Busters at several schools. I made contact with a couple publishing companies, and in November 2018, I was offered a contract to bring this book to print.

I encounter people at conferences every year who talk wistfully about wanting to present someday. When I ask why they aren't presenting, they often respond with worries of fear of rejection or, like me, the belief that they are "just" a teacher. Well, here's the deal:

"No" (typically) won't kill you.

You have your own unique story to share.

Let's address that second point first. Think through what you do well. No false modesty here, no low self-esteem. Just make a mental list of the aspects of your profession you're genuinely proud of. These are the lessons or ideas that make you light up when you talk about them. They're the ones you look forward to. If you're so inclined, you might Instagram or tweet about these lessons. Now narrow that list to your top two or three things. This is what students remember about you. Your story is in there somewhere. Think about how you do those things differently than others. How did you learn to do them well? What did you overcome? What have you learned since? What impact has it had on students? What impact has it had on you? Your story will be a boon and an inspiration to someone. Be brave enough to share it.

Ah, but that courage is hard, right? We risk so much rejection. We risk failure.

If the worst they can tell you is "no," why not try? If you don't try, life stays the same. If you're told "no," life stays the same. So what's the risk?

Much like the failure of a newly attempted activity, a "no" might mean your proposal needs to be tweaked or refined. It may mean this particular venue isn't quite right for your message. A major educational conference rejected my proposals two years in a row within the timeline I described above. Those rejections hurt, but I also knew my sessions were popular and successful with AMLE and other organizations, so my session might not have been a good fit for that particular venue. Don't let a "no" be the end of your story.

I'm so glad it wasn't the end of mine.

Thank you for being with me on this journey. I know how limited our time and resources are as educators, so the fact that you chose to spend some of that with me is humbling. I hope this time together has been beneficial and that you have found some encouragement and ideas along the way. If not, I hope you find both with some other awesome educational resource out there. We are an impressive community, we educators, so keep seeking. And share your story, so you can encourage and support someone else.

Be the magic.

Bibliography

Chapter 7

Adams, Julie. "7 Habits of Highly Effective Instructional Leaders." Speech, Columbus, OH, October 16, 2015.

Core Competencies listed at riseindiana.org.

Boredom Buster Index

ACKNOWLEDGMENTS

When I first started presenting Worksheet Busters, I paid my own way to MANY conferences. My husband never batted an eye. He has been my biggest fan for many years now. Nathan, I am where I am today because you believed in me. "Thank you" just isn't enough. At least I get to say, "I love you" instead.

When I decided I wanted to write this book, my children wanted to write books too. We spent summer afternoons piled onto the backyard hammock together, happily writing in the dappled sunshine. When I found out I got a contract, they were the first people I wanted to tell. Tovi and Oren, I hope I've shown you to be bold, be brave, and try big things. Thank you for being on this journey with me.

My dad is a journalist. I was raised with the written word. Thank you, Dad, for steeping me in language, for spending dinners talking about finding precisely the right words for your headlines. I know you've written books that sit, unpublished, somewhere in cyberspace. Publish them. Or I'll do it posthumously. But I'd rather you be around to enjoy it.

My mom earned her college degree when I was in middle school. I watched her study for hours at a time, carefully transcribing recordings of her classes. She showed me what it means to work hard for a goal, even a scary one. But one of the best things I learned from her was that failure does not have to be the end of your story. Algebra, right? Thank you, Mom, for teaching me what it looks like to work hard for something that's worth it, even when it's not easy.

I have the best friends in the whole world. They're the kind of friends that send me to a spa for a day of pampering for no other reason than that I'd never do it for myself. They're the kind of friends that clean my house and fold all my laundry when I haven't had time to take an extra breath for myself. Yeah, I have THOSE friends. I am a lucky woman. Thank you.

To the friend of my heart, Lindsay, I'm so thankful Nathan set us up on that friend date all those years ago. Your friendship is one of the greatest treasures in my life, but it's made all the richer by getting to share it with our boys. I love you, friend.

Professionally, I owe the teacher I am today to a few special people. To the first teacher to truly see me all those years ago, Mrs. Sourbeer, I hope you took your shoes off and got comfortable before reading this book. Thank you for seeing more in me than I saw in myself and for opening my eyes to how exciting learning could be.

To Miss Lorraine, I know you won't get to read this acknowledgment this side of heaven, but thank you for teaching me what dedication looks like and for never accepting less than that from me.

To Dr. Patten, Mr. and Mrs. Gearhart, Dr. Dickinson, Mr. Robbinette, Dr. Ketchen, Dr. Templar, and the rest of the faculty and staff of Johnson University, thank you for teaching me to teach children first, content second. Your lessons are with me every day.

To Sue and Chris, thank you for thinking of everything I didn't even know to think of in those early years. Your patience, wisdom, and organization saved my life, time and again.

Annie, you gave me confidence, laughter, advice, encouragement, knowledge, and more. Thank you for being my mentor and friend.

To Destiny and Sarah, thank you for sharing the title of Wonder Aide. You are both more extraordinary than you know. Destiny, don't forget the paper plate. Sarah, thank you for sharing in our mutual love for everything Office and loaded tater tots. Thank you.

To Christine, Erin, Todd, Michael, and the rest of my amazing #mschat PLN, you all inspire me to be more and more each day. Every teacher would benefit from a network of support, encouragement, and ideas like I've found with you. Jacquie and Brian, thank you for Lyft rides and good food paid for by the hardest-won gift card I've ever encountered.

Dru, thank you for your work with AMLE and for connecting me to opportunities to do more. Always, behind it all, is the amazing Dena, connecting all the dots, making everything happen. Thank you.

To Dave and Shelley, thank you for not making me feel weird for reaching out with what I felt was a crazy idea. Thank you for letting me be bold.

To every student I've had over these years, thank you. Thank you for being patient with my epic failures, game to try my wild new ideas, and willing to develop a culture of trust, safety, respect, and fun together. You all have made my job a sheer pleasure. How lucky am I to have had you!

And to the parents who hand their children over to us every day, thank you for trusting us with your children. That's a hard, sometimes scary thing. We believe in your children and in the greatness that's possible with them. Thank you for letting us partner with you.

To the many wonderful educators I've met over the years, presenting Worksheet Busters across the country, thank you for playing with paper airplanes and Learning Spheres with me. Thank you for helping me see just how magic this can be.

MORE FROM

Dave Burgess Consulting, Inc.

Since 2012, DBCI has been publishing books that inspire and equip educators to be their best. For more information on our DBCI titles or to purchase bulk orders for your school, district, or book study, visit **DaveBurgessconsulting.com/DBCIbooks**.

More from the *Like a PIRATE*™ Series

Teach Like a PIRATE by Dave Burgess

eXPlore Like a Pirate by Michael Matera

Learn Like a Pirate by Paul Solarz

Play Like a Pirate by Quinn Rollins

Run Like a Pirate by Adam Welcome

Lead Like a PIRATE™ Series

Lead Like a PIRATE by Shelley Burgess and Beth Houf

Balance Like a Pirate by Jessica Cabeen, Jessica Johnson, and Sarah Johnson

Lead beyond Your Title by Nili Bartley

Lead with Culture by Jay Billy

Lead with Literacy by Mandy Ellis

Leadership & School Culture

Culturize by Jimmy Casas

Escaping the School Leader's Dunk Tank by Rebecca Coda and Rick Jetter

From Teacher to Leader by Starr Sackstein
The Innovator's Mindset by George Couros
Kids Deserve It! by Todd Nesloney and Adam Welcome
Let Them Speak by Rebecca Coda and Rick Jetter
The Limitless School by Abe Hege and Adam Dovico
The Pepper Effect by Sean Gaillard
The Principled Principal by Jeffrey Zoul and Anthony McConnell
Relentless by Hamish Brewer
The Secret Solution by Todd Whitaker, Sam Miller, and Ryan Donlan
Start. Right. Now. by Todd Whitaker, Jeffrey Zoul, and Jimmy Casas
Stop. Right. Now. by Jimmy Casas and Jeffrey Zoul
They Call Me "Mr. De" by Frank DeAngelis
Unmapped Potential by Julie Hasson and Missy Lennard
Word Shift by Joy Kirr
Your School Rocks by Ryan McLane and Eric Lowe

Technology & Tools

50 Things You Can Do with Google Classroom by Alice Keeler and Libbi Miller
50 Things to Go Further with Google Classroom by Alice Keeler and Libbi Miller
140 Twitter Tips for Educators by Brad Currie, Billy Krakower, and Scott Rocco
Block Breaker by Brian Aspinall
Code Breaker by Brian Aspinall
Google Apps for Littles by Christine Pinto and Alice Keeler
Master the Media by Julie Smith
Shake Up Learning by Kasey Bell

Social LEADia by Jennifer Casa-Todd
Teaching Math with Google Apps by Alice Keeler and Diana Herrington
Teachingland by Amanda Fox and Mary Ellen Weeks

Teaching Methods & Materials

All 4s and 5s by Andrew Sharos
The Classroom Chef by John Stevens and Matt Vaudrey
Ditch That Homework by Matt Miller and Alice Keeler
Ditch That Textbook by Matt Miller
Don't Ditch That Tech by Matt Miller, Nate Ridgway, and Angelia Ridgway
EDrenaline Rush by John Meehan
Educated by Design by Michael Cohen, The Tech Rabbi
The EduProtocol Field Guide by Marlena Hebern and Jon Corippo
The EduProtocol Field Guide: Book 2 by Marlena Heburn and Jon Corippo
Instant Relevance by Denis Sheeran
LAUNCH by John Spencer and A.J. Juliani
Make Learning MAGICAL by Tisha Richmond
Pure Genius by Don Wettrick
The Revolution by Darren Ellwein and Derek McCoy
Shift This! by Joy Kirr
Spark Learning by Ramsey Musallam
Sparks in the Dark by Travis Crowder and Todd Nesloney
Table Talk Math by John Stevens
The Wild Card by Hope and Wade King
The Writing on the Classroom Wall by Steve Wyborney

Inspiration, Professional Growth & Personal Development

Be REAL by Tara Martin

Be the One for Kids by Ryan Sheehy

Creatively Productive by Lisa Johnson

The EduNinja Mindset by Jennifer Burdis

Empower Our Girls by Lynmara Colón and Adam Welcome

The Four O'Clock Faculty by Rich Czyz

How Much Water Do We Have? by Pete and Kris Nunweiler

P Is for Pirate by Dave and Shelley Burgess

A Passion for Kindness by Tamara Letter

The Path to Serendipity by Allyson Apsey

Sanctuaries by Dan Tricarico

Shattering the Perfect Teacher Myth by Aaron Hogan

Stories from Webb by Todd Nesloney

Talk to Me by Kim Bearden

Teach Me, Teacher by Jacob Chastain

TeamMakers by Laura Robb and Evan Robb

Through the Lens of Serendipity by Allyson Apsey

The Zen Teacher by Dan Tricarico

Children's Books

Beyond Us by Aaron Polansky

Cannonball In by Tara Martin

Dolphins in Trees by Aaron Polansky

I Want to Be a Lot by Ashley Savage

The Princes of Serendip by Allyson Apsey

Zom-Be a Design Thinker by Amanda Fox

Bring Katie Powell to Your Next School or District Event

Topics include:

Worksheet Busters (60-90 minute workshop session)

Learn to turn ordinary worksheets into active, collaborative, memorable learning experiences that can be used over and over again for virtually any content with little to no preparation. Imagine the response when you dump 30 colorful balls in the middle of your room, tell students to turn their worksheets into paper airplanes, or unfurl a giant board game across your floor. Curious? They will be too. And they'll want to come back for more tomorrow.

Lecture Busters (60-90 minute workshop session)

Given that even most adults can pay attention to a lecture just minutes at a time, it's no surprise our students "zone out" sometimes. Lecture Busters are engaging, challenging, thought-provoking checks for understanding we can use to break up our lectures, get students thinking about what we have taught, and provide useful feedback to guide our teaching. These Lecture Busters are easy to have on hand to use spur-of-the-moment or as a planned part of our teaching routine. Bust the lecture routine and get students engaged!

Homework Busters (60-90 minute workshop session)

Homework is a hot topic these days. Whether you give homework or not, you probably still find yourself needing to provide some kind of meaningful feedback on student work. But often students look only as far as their score and consider the assignment done. Consider ways to keep the learning going beyond the grade as students analyze their errors, evaluate their learning, and make connections to understand the content far beyond the bounds of the original assignment.

Teaching Beyond the Desk (60-90 minute workshop session)

Worksheet Busters are easy, effective activity frameworks that transform ordinary worksheets into engaging, meaningful learning experiences. Learn several of these easy-to-replicate activities and how to design your own Worksheet Busters to engage students within your own teaching style and content.

"No" (Probably) Won't Kill You (Keynote presentation)

Have you ever considered presenting, writing, or taking on a new challenge? What holds you back? In this keynote presentation, Katie shares her journey as encouragement and inspiration to not fear "No" and to dare to do big things.

And more. Sessions can be combined or customized to meet your specific needs.

Contact Katie through her website at
teachbeyondthedesk.com

About the Author

Katie Powell began teaching in 2005 and has served as a special education teacher, Title 1 teacher, instructional coach, and classroom teacher. This focus on providing interventions for struggling students led to the development of strategies that leverage curiosity and fun to engage students while driving learning deeper. While serving as an instructional coach, Katie fine-tuned these strategies to be easily deployable in virtually any instructional setting without sacrificing teachers' already-limited time or money. Katie has presented her popular Worksheet Busters and Lecture Busters sessions at conferences and districts across the country. Katie believes in respecting the expertise of teachers and shares her creative process so they can address engagement and depth in their classrooms within their own teaching styles and content.

Katie lives in Indiana with her husband, Nathan, and sons, Tovi and Oren. She teaches sixth grade reading and language arts. Connect with Katie on Twitter @beyond_the_desk.

Made in the USA
Middletown, DE
26 November 2019